THE LIGHTHOUSE

CHARLOTTE WEBB

NENE PUBLISHING

CHAPTER ONE

Emily woke with a gasp, sweat beaded on her face. Tiredness was immediately replaced by terror. Another nightmare. She squinted at the small digital clock sitting on the bedside table, 2.22 am. She steadied her breathing. "Just a nightmare," she said to herself, "just another nightmare."

The hard wooden floors were cold underfoot, a soothing feeling that radiated through her body as she dodged the stacks of boxes on her way to the bathroom; over a month and she still hadn't completely unpacked. She flicked the switch on the bathroom wall and stood staring at herself in the mirror. Her blonde hair was dishevelled, and the bags under her bright blue eyes emphasised a look of wear. She thought she'd find youthfulness in the move. The fresh start, the change of pace, several notches down from the demanding speed of her old life, and it seemed to be having the opposite effect.

"Just have to get through the adjustment period," she said to herself, and turned the antiquated brass knob of the old tap. Cold water ran in a slow, steady stream as she splashed her face, rinsing the sweat away. She buried her face in the towel and held it there as she relived the horror of the nightmare. "Just let it go, don't think about it" As she dropped the towel from her face and opened her eyes, she was in darkness, "What the hell", she was startled by the buzzing and the sudden flickering on of the old Edison style lightbulb in ceiling light. It blinded her for a second before turning off again.

"Damn it," she screeched, and then caught her breath, "that's it. These lights are getting fixed today."

She threw the switch off with frustration. The lights were an ongoing issue, amongst other things, things that she put down to the cottage being old and poorly maintained over the years. Things like doors that would get jammed shut, then slowly creak open by themselves, leaking water pipes that would leave small puddles here and there throughout the cottage. Small things but they needed to be fixed. The cottages had been built in 1809 for the crews who manned the lighthouse. This went on for 180 years until the last crew left in 1989 when the lighthouse was finally automated. The cottages had stood empty for several decades before they were then sold off individually for holiday letting. She quickly distracted herself from the frustration of the general disarray of the small house and welcomed the smell of the fresh coffee she had begun brewing. Multitasking, she settled into the routine of readying herself for her day. Even the slow pace of the small town on the isle of Anglesey in North Wales couldn't break her of her rushed morning habits. She checked the time on her phone, not even seven a.m. yet, and she was all set for her day. She capitalized on the extra hour that she had before she had to open the coffee shop and embraced the frigid morning air as she stepped outside of her little cottage.

Her little cottage was one of four that were all connected in a row extending out from the base of the old lighthouse, perched on the edge of a sheer cliff overlooking the Irish Sea. Hers was the one immediately connected to the lighthouse. The three other cottages remained largely empty and were rented out as holiday homes in the season. Her coffee steamed in the cold sea air, and she watched the white wisps get pulled away by the ocean breeze. It was a blustery day, and the early morning was cold. The noise of the gulls as they blew around was captivating and she couldn't quite believe she was here. She had longed for this life for years, and the timing had been perfect. After separating from her husband, and with her daughter Daisy off at university, there was no better time for a fresh start. Years of her existence as a high-level executive in London had finally paid off, and her dream of living a calm, more simple life was almost realised. She took it all in, she had made the right decision, everything would settle down given a little bit of time.

Back inside her warm cozy cottage, she placed the mug in the little kitchen sink and the frustration of the morning left her. She gathered her things, gathered herself, and headed out. "Shit," she murmured at the old, wood plank door. Her car keys weren't hanging on the small nail next to the door, the place where she always hung them. Things going missing were a thing of Emily's nightmares, especially when she had somewhere to be, and it was beginning to be an all-too-common occurrence as of late. Frantically, she began searching. The cottage was small and consisted only of a small kitchen/dining room, a larger living room overlooking the stunning view of the cliffs and sea and a bathroom on the ground floor. Up the old wooden stairs now painted white were two good sized double bedrooms, one of which had a small ensuite which Emily had chosen as hers- not because of the ensuite, but because it had the very best view. The other bedroom had a huge hatch to the attic, which she thought would make the perfect painting studio one day.

Emily tore through the opened boxes, emptied the laundry basket, checked the pockets of her coat, the jeans she had worn yesterday, and even went so far as to check senseless places like the fridge and under her bed, none of which turned up the keys. The frustration returned tenfold, and she resigned herself to walking to the little café she now ran. It was a brisk 30-minute walk along the coastal path she had been told about by the estate agent on her first visit to the cottage at the end of the previous summer. She was warned not to use it in the depths of the winter though, as the wind could whip the waves up and over the path and people had been washed into the sea. But it was summer, and she often walked if she didn't have to pick up anything on her way there or back. Her little row of cottages was set about 3 miles outside of the town by road, but the walk along the coastal path was around a mile and a half; lovely when the sun was shining, but this morning it was blustery, and rain threatened her on a day she needed to get shopping on the way home. Opening the front door, Emily caught the glint of her keys, hanging on the small, rusted hook, just where they always were. She snatched them and shook her head in disbelief as she shut and locked the door. Finally in the car, she dialled Daisy.

"Hey mum, how's the lighthouse?", Daisy's bubbly attitude was a welcome familiarity.

"Just lovely," Emily couldn't mask her remaining frustration.

"I can hear something is wrong, what is it?" Daisy asked.

"Nothing really," Emily took a deep breath, "just a disturbed sleep and frustrating morning is all."

"Still having nightmares, are you?"

Emily sighed, "Yep, I had another one last night. They're horrific Daisy."

"What was it this time?"

"There was a woman, a tragically beautiful woman, kneeling right in front of me. She looked terrified, Daisy, pale and thin and crying. She had her hands up to her face, like she was afraid of me, like I was going to hit her or something."

"Hmm," Daisy pondered for a moment, "well, they're just nightmares. I'm sure there's some psychologist who could explain about how the woman represents you etc., but honestly, I think you just need to relax a little. That was the whole point of your moving, remember? Try and enjoy yourself. How's your coffee shop doing?"

Emily sighed, "maybe you're right. The coffee shop is wonderful. Running it is so different than what I'm used to. I'm certainly a far cry from making millions, but it's actually fun. I can't remember ever having fun at work."

"That's amazing mum. This is a huge change for you. It's just going to take some time to get used to everything, you know?"

"I know. How's university?"

"I love it, I really do. Honestly though, I can't wait to come see you."

"I can't wait either. Listen I'm just pulling up to the shop now, I'll give you a call later, ok?"

"Sounds good mum, I love you."

"I love you too." Emily hangs up the phone as she pulls into her usual parking spot.

The coffee shop was a quaint old Tudor building, the outside beamed and pained sky blue. In one of the two big bay windows closest to the door, a sign advertised a myriad of coffee, hot chocolate and tea varieties and a full menu of hot food and cakes. The sign had been beautifully handwritten and painted by Emily. Inside the shop, she set to work getting things ready for the steady stream of regular morning customers who frequented the spot. Just as she was pouring coffee grounds into one of the filters, she jumped at the sound of a knock on one of the glass windows, sending a fine, brown sand through the air. In a flurry, she turned to see Shelly stood at the window, wearing a surprised look on her face.

Shelly's bright pink hair and beaming smile quashed any annoyance Emily had, and she unlocked the door. She was a young lady, and full of energy, even more so after having just completed a degree in History getting a first-class honors. She planned to travel for a year, something she constantly reminded Emily about, but first needed to get some money in, hence her working in the coffee shop for the summer season. In the last few weeks, Shelly had really grown on Emily, and she wasn't looking forward to the day she turned in her apron.

"Good morning, Boss." Shelly saluted Emily. This had become her greeting for Emily ever since hearing about the massive corporation she ran back in London. Emily couldn't help but smile.

"Good morning, Shelly."

She broke her stance, setting to work cleaning the spilled grounds, "awfully jumpy this morning, aren't we?"

"Sorry," Emily replied, "it's just been a bit of rough morning."

"Oh no, really, please don't apologise," Shelly's voice was always so joyful, "is everything alright?"

"Yeah," Emily paused, "just more electrical problems at the cottage. I'm finally ready to get someone in there to fix some of these things."

"Electrical problems," Shelly said sarcastically, "sure."

"Shelly, I've told you before, and I'll tell you again, it's just an old house that's all. There's no poltergeist or ghost or any of that other fictional nonsense."

Shelly rolled her big, bright green eyes.

"Now, didn't you say you know someone who

could come fix some of this stuff?" Emily quickly changed the subject, annoyed.

"Oh, totally I do, here," Shelly thumbs through her phone momentarily, and scribbles a number from it onto a small sticky note, "this is Danny's number. He can fix literally anything, give him a call."

"Thanks, I'll do that."

Shelly smiles at Emily slyly, "he's not too bad looking either, now that I think of it."

"I'll keep that in mind," Emily laughed, "now let's get opened up."

The morning went by in a flash of bustling customers, and after the lunchtime rush when things had settled down, Emily called Danny. In a quick exchange, Danny agreed to meet Emily at her cottage later that afternoon to have a look.

That afternoon Emily arrived home to see a large van parked outside of the cottage, with a long ladder perched on a rack on the top, a shred of an old orange tee-shirt tied to the end. Emily could see a man in the driver's seat, with shaggy hair dangling freely to his shoulders, his face hidden behind a thick, unkempt beard. A rolled-up sleeve revealed a muscley forearm. *This must be Danny*, Emily thought as she parked her car and approached the van.

"Excuse me, do you happen to be Danny?" Emily called out.

The door of the van creaked when it opened and was followed by the hollow sound of the steel door being shut with some force. The man smoothed his shirt before turning to greet Emily, his brown eyes full of kindness, surrounded with smile lines. He beamed a handsome smile at her and reached out his hand.

"Danny Callaway," he said through a poorly disguised smile, "you must be Emily."

"I am," Emily welcomed the unfamiliar roughness of his handshake, "thank you for coming out so quickly."

"Not a problem at all," Danny eyed over the little row of cottages, "what needs fixing?"

"Well," Emily paused for a moment, "quite a few things, to be honest. Some of the lights flicker and make loud buzzing sounds sometimes. There are some pipes that are leaking on occasion. Doors stick sometimes, too."

"Sounds like quite a list," Danny chuckled, "let's have a look. Which cottage is yours?"

"This one right at the base of the lighthouse," Emily pointed and began walking towards her little cottage.

At the front door, Emily turned her key to release the deadbolt lock and turned the old decorative knob. She pushed gently on the front door at first and, after a failure to generate any movement, she began pushing a bit harder. Three hard thrusts and still nothing.

Emily sighed heavily, "see what I mean?"

"Yeah, that would get old pretty quick I bet," Danny chuckled and gestured at the door, "may I?"

"Have it," Emily said, stepping aside.

Danny gripped the darkened steel knob, turning it one way and then the other meticulously, his ear pressed against the hard-wooden door, listening inventively.

"Sounds like the mechanisms releasing." Danny then tried a few forceful pushes on the door before resorting to using his body weight to force the front door open. "Damn," he said, pondering for a moment, "That happen often?"

"That's the worst it's been," Emily said, wide-eyed, thinking that if a man Danny's size, as well built as he was struggled, there was a good chance she would have never got the door to budge, "but it's not just this one, the other doors in the house get stuck too sometimes."

Standing in the doorway, Danny carefully eyed

the framework of the door as he moved it slowly on its antiquated hinges, examining the space between the door jamb and the slab as he moved it almost to a completely closed position, but not quite all the way, hesitant it might get stuck again.

"Hmmm," he thought out loud, "probably just swelling from the moisture in the air, I can shave a little bit off it, that should give it a little more clearance and keep it from getting stuck."

"Oh," Emily bore a look of relief, glad that there was some remedy for the sticking doors, "perfect."

Danny smiled, "let's take a look at what else you're having issues with."

Emily nodded in agreement, "just ignore all of the boxes and the messiness."

"Just moved in?" Danny inquired, glancing around the room.

"It's been a process," Emily chuckled, and began showing Danny around.

Emily walked Danny through the old cottage, showing him where the various water spots had appeared, the buzzing lights, the doors that drifted open and shut on their own. Danny had pulled a small notebook and a carpenter's pencil from his breast pocket. Anywhere Emily would describe an issue, Danny would stop, inspecting the area with diligence and scribble some words in his little pocket notebook. Emily admired his attentiveness, and appreciated that he appeared to believe her statements, even though all the doors worked fine, there was no water on the floor, and the lights didn't so much as blink once.

"Well, it sounds like we definitely have our work cut out for us," Danny said, showing his slightly crooked white teeth behind a large smile, "but we'll get it all squared up for you. Old places like this usually come with their fair share of issues, and these little cottages are very old."

"They really are," Emily smiled, "It's part of their charm, one of the reasons I fell in love with them."

Danny took a long look around, admiring the antique fixtures, the dark, solid wooden floors, "You know, I think these are the cottages where my great, great grandfather lived."

"No, really, which one?"

"I'm not sure, but I remember my dad used to talk about coming up to these cottages all the time when he was a kid. I did a bit of work in the cottage at the other end, which happened to have similar issues to this one. They tried renting it out, but it didn't work out, so they sold it fairly quickly. I'm not sure who owns it now. But I can see why my old Dad loved coming up here."

"It's beautiful here," Emily said earnestly, "I absolutely love it. Seeing the sea every morning is worth all the little headaches, undoubtedly."

Danny laughed, "well, hopefully we'll get rid of some of these headaches for you."

"Thank you again," Emily's voice was full of sincerity.

"Not a problem," Danny said confidently, walking towards the front door.

Emily followed him outside, cursing at herself for her momentary forgetfulness as she pulled the front door shut. She blushed with embarrassment when Danny turned around.

"Should I get a sledgehammer?" He joked.

Emily watched as he dug through the rear of his van, wondering if he might be serious about the sledgehammer comment. A few moments passed before he emerged with a canvas bag of tools, and a small saw of some kind.

"Let me get this front door fixed now and I'll be out of your hair in no time."

"Oh," Emily looked at her watch, "you don't have to start right now. It's getting late, I don't want to keep you from your family or anything."

"No family, just me, and you are only keeping me from my Friday fish and chips. I wouldn't be able to sleep tonight wondering if you accidentally got yourself trapped in there. Unless I'll be disrupting you and your family?"

"It's just me here," Emily let out a small sigh, "I don't mind at all, I just didn't want to put you out is all."

The front door opened perfectly easily this time, Danny just smiled and set to work. The usual quietness of the cottage was replaced by the sounds of buzzing and brushing, and the occasional noise of Danny's breath as he blew away shavings. Emily made him some tea and busied herself with unpacking, ensuring not to be the type of person that would hover, or interrupt someone doing their job, except when she caught the scent of burning tobacco. She waited for a break in the loud humming of Danny's saw.

"Hey Danny, I hate to ask, but would you mind smoking away from the house a little, while the door is open? I'm just not a big fan of the smoke, it makes me cough."

"Oh, I don't smoke, but I can smell it too, I thought it was you"

"I'm sorry," Emily exclaimed with embarrassment, "I thought it had to be you."

"Interesting," Danny's eyes become curious as he breathes the scent in through his nose, "I definitely smell it. Almost like pipe smoke, I'd say. Are you burning a candle or something?"

Emily shakes her head, a puzzled look on her face. Danny leans through the front door, glancing around the dimming parking area.

"Nobody out here," he shrugged, "maybe someone next door?"

"The other cottages have been empty," Emily pulled a hooded sweatshirt on over her head; the air cooling in the darkening evening, "let me go and check though."

Danny finished cleaning up after his work, staying outside to keep an eye on Emily, as she went door to door to all three of the attached cottages in the row, to no answer. At each cottage, after several knocks, she would cup her hands around her eyes, peering through the front window. Danny, collecting his tools, noticed the increasing presence of the scent.

"Anyone here?" He called to Emily, as she was walking back.

"Nobody," She called back, "as far as I can tell."

"That smell is getting pretty strong," Danny commented, "you might want to make sure nothing is burning. Mind if I check the electrical stuff?"

"By all means," Emily looked worried, "please do. Thank you so much."

Danny set to finding the electrical panel, feeling for any warming wires, and did the same at all the light switches and outlets he could find. Meanwhile, Emily double checked the stove, the coffee pot, and carefully examined every room for any signs of something burning. Neither of them found anything. Now the smell of pipe tobacco permeated every room in the house. Back at the entryway, they exchanged equally questioning looks.

"Must be the wind carrying the smell in," Danny concluded, "It'll probably clear up once this door is shut."

"Hopefully," Emily conceded, her voice doubtful.

"Well," Danny opened and closed the door several times, again examining the small space between the jamb and the slab, "this one's fixed I think."

"Thank god," Emily let out a long sigh, "I really appreciate it."

Danny gathered his tools, "of course."

Emily followed Danny to his van, closing the door behind her.

"How much do I owe you?" She asked.

"First one's on me," He smiled, "don't worry about it."

"I can't let you do that."

"I insist. I'll come back tomorr-" Danny stopped short of finishing his sentence.

Emily noticed Danny staring at her little cottage, and immediately she realised what had grabbed his attention so abruptly. Through the curtains they could see the flashing of a light from the second story of the little house; on and off in a steady punctuated rhythm. Danny and Emily stood, watching the light pulsing, equally puzzled.

Danny broke the silence, "is that what you were talking about with the flickering lights?"

"I haven't seen it do that before, it's usually more of a quick flickering, not really on and off like that."

"Let me see if I have a bulb in my van," Danny's voice couldn't quite mask his doubt.

Danny pulled a bulb from a box in his pickup. Emily followed him up the thick wooden steps, creaking heavily under the weight of Danny's boots. Inside of the room, Danny flicked the switch off and back on, the light illuminated without issue. He repeated the process several times before leaving the switch off and handing Emily a little pocket flashlight to hold as he replaced the bulb. After the bulb was replaced, Danny left the switch off, and brushed his hands together in a motion, signifying he was satisfied with the resolution.

"Well, that should be that."

"I can't thank you enough," Emily reiterated her gratitude, and followed him to his van.

"Same time tomorrow then?" Danny asked.

"I'll see you then," she smiled.

The engine roared to life as Danny started his van. Emily began walking back, distracted by her phone, when she was startled by the sound of Danny's tires sliding on the gravel parking area as he slammed on his brakes. Danny jumped out of the van leaving the door open as he approached Emily.

"Did you forget something?" Emily asked, still slightly stunned from the commotion.

Danny pointed at the second story window the curtains illuminated.

"I swear I left that light off when we came down." Danny's voice was firm.

"When that light was going off and on before, I was going to tell you I was certain it should have been off. I never go up there. I thought maybe I was losing it."

Emily followed Danny back up to the second story. By the time they reached the small room on the second floor, the light was off, and Danny confirmed the switch was in the off position. He tested the light a few times and found it to be working just as it should.

"What would cause that?" Emily asked nervously.

"I'm not sure," Danny paused, thinking to himself.

"Should I be worried?" Emily asked.

"No, I'm sure it's jus-"

Before Danny could finish his sentence, the light suddenly flashed on, and immediately off again.

"Shit," Emily shrieked in terror.

Danny doubled over, catching his breath.

"Christ," he laughed, "that scared the bloody hell out of me. You might have bigger problems that I thought."

Danny looked at Emily, still visibly shaken from the scare. He placed his hand on her shoulder, heavy and warm.

"I'll just take the bulb out for now," a very slight shakiness detectable in his voice, "I'll get it fixed tomorrow. It's probably just a bad switch, I'll pick one up first thing in the morning."

Emily found herself comforted by the sureness in his voice, and the perfectly logical explanation. Danny removed the lightbulb, handing it to Emily with a smile. Emily watched Danny leave with a wave from the window of his van as he pulled away. Despite her level-headedness, and the reassurance from Danny, she found herself to still be uneasy. She poured a large glass of wine and tried to distract herself with some mindless television. She lay in bed, plagued by a feeling of nervousness she couldn't shake, and the thought that, despite having only met him a few hours ago, she wished he would have offered to stay through the night.

CHAPTER
TWO

"Here you are," Emily said sweetly, handing the coffee to Danny, steam slipping out of the hole in the black plastic lid.

"I appreciate it," Danny smiled, sipping on the hot coffee, "amazing as always."

"Well, it's not overly complicated," Emily said teasingly, "you know we have these menus full of interesting things to try. Life doesn't always have to be just plain black coffee."

"Very true, very true," Danny chuckled, "maybe tomorrow I'll let you choose for me."

"Deal," Emily replied, boasting her confidence with a crooked smile.

"Very well," Danny called out, raising his cup as if in the gesture of a toast as he pushed through the glass front door, "I'll see you later this afternoon."

Emily smiled, her cheeks a rosy-red as she watched Danny cross the road outside of the little café to his van that she had become accustomed to seeing almost every afternoon after work over the last week as he worked on repairs around Emily's little cottage.

Shelly winked, "You guys are getting on well then?"

"He's very friendly and kind" Emily smiled

"I think he may have more than friendship on his mind the way he grinned at you"

"Shelly!" Emily giggled, "I doubt that"

"It's sooooo obvious you're into each other!"

"No, it's not like that-I don't think," Emily said

"I think you will find it is!" laughed Shelly

"Anyway, how's he doing up there? Getting everything fixed?"

"He's certainly trying. He seems very good at his job, but there's a few things he's struggling with. The lights still flickering and things like that," Emily said, trying to sound as nonchalant as she could. Emily could read Shelly's face like a book- and it read a look of *I told you so*. Emily busied herself with a customer who had walked in before Shelly could get a word in.

That afternoon, Emily arrived home to her little seaside cottage to Danny rummaging through his van, packing his tool bag with various tools and parts for the day's repairs. The air was cool and crisp, and the steady breeze brought with it the scent of salty ocean air, which Emily welcomed. Emily watched from her car for a moment, admiring the muscles that articulated in his forearms with each movement of his hands.

"What are we fixing today?" Emily called as she approached the van.

"Well, I've been thinking about the lights, and the only thing I can come up with is that the wiring must be faulty," Danny pulled a heavy spool of electrical wire towards the end of the of van, "so, I think I'm going to have to try and replace quite a bit."

"That sounds like an awful lot of work," Emily replied pitifully.

"It won't be so bad," Danny smiled and winked, "It's hardly work with such lovely company anyway."

Emily returned the smile with a little blush and

followed Danny into the house. The hours ticked by as Emily read, distracted by the commotion of Danny's drilling and the sounds of wires sliding behind the old plaster walls, and Danny's brilliant smile whenever he passed through the room. She had started cooking when the house grew silent. Figuring that Danny must be done for the night, she steeled herself, building confidence in what she was preparing to ask him.

"Well," Danny said, entering the little living room where Emily was sitting, "if that doesn't fix it, I don't know what will."

"I can't thank you enough for doing all of this work," Emily said cheerfully.

"Thank me when it works," Danny chuckled.

"I mean it." Emily said earnestly.

"Same time tomorrow?"

Emily looked at her watch. "Actually, I was going to ask if you would be interested in staying for dinner tonight? I've scarcely paid you for all the work that you've been doing. I figured it's the least I could do."

"I couldn't possibly. I don't want to put you out." Danny's smile grew wider than ever.

"Nonsense," Emily replied, "I've almost finished

and there's more than I could possibly eat myself. Is spaghetti alright?"

"That sounds lovely," Danny replied.

"Then it's settled."

"I'll get my tools packed up," Danny said, and then looked at his hands, "Would you mind if I had a shower, I've got clean clothes in the van?"

"Of course not, make yourself at home, you know where the fresh towels are by now."

Emily returned to the kitchen as Danny gathered his things. Emily listened to his movements and basked in the pride she had in her confidence. She couldn't wait to tell Shelly tomorrow; she could already hear the excitement in her voice.

"Bloody hell!" Danny's voice boomed through the house, causing Emily to nearly drop the large pot of boiling water.

"Is everything alright?" Emily called, hurrying to set the pot down and make her way towards the bathroom. In the little hallway, she recognized the issue in an instant. Under the bathroom door, she could see the flickering illumination of the bathroom light. She knocked on the door, "are you alright?"

The knob of the door rattled. "Oh, hell", Danny

stated in a flat tone; defeated. "Now I can't open the door."

"I'll try and help. I'll push and you pull. Are you ready?"

"Let's give it a shot. One, two, three."

Emily turned the knob and pushed, with all her weight, against the door. On the other side of the wooden slab, Danny pulled with all his might. Danny's grip slipped, sending him stumbling backwards into the wall. Emily ceased her pushing, letting out a long, exasperated sigh.

"What are we going to do now?" Emily's voice was becoming shaky.

"Let me see here," Danny's voice remained steady and confident, he chuckled, "it would be a lot easier to think if this light would stop."

Emily looked at the floor, she could see the light was flickering, on and off with a relentless speed, "I'll slide my phone under the door, then you can just turn the light off for now."

"That's the thing," Danny replied, "I already turned the switch off."

"I don't understand, what would cause that?" Emily asked, her voice full of nervousness now.

"Let's get one thing figured out at a time," Danny chuckled, "I'm going to slide my keys under the door. My tool bag is sitting on the floor of the passenger side of my van. Could you go and grab it?"

"Of course," Emily said, pulling the keys from under the door, "I'll be right back."

"I won't have moved," Danny laughed.

Emily hurried to the van, moving so quickly that she nearly slipped on a small puddle of water just in front of the main door. She cursed under her breath, *damn old cottage.* She was mindful of the water on her way back to the bathroom with Danny's tool bag. Emily could hear Danny continuing to jiggle the knob and yank on the door.

"I'm back, what do I do now?"

"In one of the side pockets should be a screwdriver, the one with a flat tip. I need you to see if you can slide it under the door."

Emily frantically searched the pockets of Danny's tool bag, finding the flat tipped screwdriver, "Found it!".

"Fantastic," Danny replied, "now see if you can slide it under."

Emily placed the screwdriver on the floor, against that bottom of the door, and attempted to push it under. The screwdriver became wedged, not quite fitting. Emily strained her fingers, using them to try and force it under, eventually resorting to using her fist as a hammer, pounding it through. Danny immediately grabbed the screwdriver. Emily could hear the sound of metal on metal as Danny tried to pry the mechanism loose from the latch. Emily sat silently, not wanting to distract him. A few minutes felt like an eternity before Danny finally broke the silence. "Shit."

Emily's panic hit full throttle. "What? What is it?"

"I can't get it, and this damn flashing light isn't helping."

"Can you take the bulb out?" Emily asked.

"Now why didn't I think of that?" Danny asked, humor finding its way back into his tone.

Emily listened to Danny shuffling around, and a few moments later, the room went black for a moment before Emily could see the white light of her phone bouncing off the floor.

"Alright then," Danny said, "let's see here."

The metallic sound of Danny fiddling with the door handle resumed and suddenly the door opened.

"You got it!" Emily exclaimed relieved.

"I guess," Danny said, a puzzled look on his face, "I don't know what I did, though. It just worked suddenly."

"Who cares? At least you're not stuck anymore."

Danny laughed, "Still offering that dinner?"

"Of course," Emily smiled. "What am I going to do about the door?"

Danny eyed it over for a minute, turning the knob to make sure that the latching mechanism disengaged properly, even going so far as to open and close the door several times, ensuring that everything functioned as it should.

"I think I should replace the handle. Maybe even the door too."

"Alright," Emily nodded in agreement, "and what about the light?"

"Honestly? I'm not really sure at this point. I'll put the bulb back in and see what it does I suppose. It has a new switch, new wiring. Maybe something's happening with that old fixture. Let me think on it. In the meantime, I wouldn't close this door, just in case. I'll fix this one first tomorrow afternoon."

"Alright," Emily said, sounding defeated.

Danny placed his large hand on her shoulder, "It'll be alright, we'll get it figured it out."

Emily smiled wearily.

While Emily set the plates, Danny reinstalled the light bulb, which now remained steadily illuminated when the switch was on, and completely dark when the switch was off. He shook his head, puzzled. Emily and Danny enjoyed dinner together, keeping the conversation light, talking about the weather, the coffee shop and Danny's work on the cottage. The conversation continued as Emily rinsed the dishes and loaded the machine while Danny poured them each a glass of red wine. As Emily and Danny settled back at the table, a loud noise boomed through the house. The noise was sharp and piercing, like the crack of a large tree splitting under the pressure of a high wind. The house went completely dark.

"What the fuck was that?" Emily shrieked.

Danny fumbled for his phone, quickly glancing around the room with it, coming to a rest on Emily's face, shimmering with tears.

"I'm not sure," Danny said, "I will check the fuse box" Moments later Emily heard Danny calling from the under-stair cupboard "All fine here, maybe a pole went down on a power line or something."

Emily followed Danny to the kitchen window, where they both looked out at a star-filled sky and the silhouette of the tree in the garden of the cottage was stone still, not a breath of wind.

"Let's take a drive down the road, see what

knocked out the power out. What do you say?" Danny's voice remained calm and sure.

Danny led the way to the front door. No sooner had Danny placed a foot over the threshold then all the lights in the house flashed back on. They paused in the entry way, stunned by the sudden return of power.

Danny broke the silence with a laugh, "well, that was strange."

Emily let out a long sigh, "maybe Shelly's right," she chuckled, "maybe this old cottage really is haunted."

Danny eyed her, "you don't really believe that do you? There's no such thing as ghosts."

"I know," Emily forced a laugh, before blurting out "but would you stay here tonight?" Immediately, Emily regretted asking, and tried to back pedal before Danny could answer, "never mind. I'm sorry, you barely know me. I don't know what I was thinking, I swear I don't. I'm just being childish."

"You're not being childish," Danny reassured her, "and I don't mind staying at all."

"Really? Are you sure?"

"I'm positive. How about that glass of wine?"

"That sounds lovely," Emily replied with a weary smile.

They shared a glass of wine and sat out in the night air, listening to the waves crash against the cliffs and watching the lights of the ships in the bay bounce in the rhythmic motion of the sea. The comfort of Danny's presence warmed Emily, even more than the wine.

"So, what brought you to Anglesey anyway?" Danny asked.

"Oh, I fell in love with this place years ago. I came here on a trip once, and I remember seeing these little cottages and thinking, this is where I want to be. Then everything just fell into place, you know? Daisy was off to university, Chris and I separated, and I was ready for a career change. When I saw one of the cottages were for sale, I jumped at it. Now here I am. What about you? Ever entertain thoughts of a different life?"

"Me?" Danny laughed, "Never. I love it here, I always have. I love the quietness of it, the ocean."

Emily raised her glass, "To Anglesey."

"To new lives and old lives," Danny smiled.

They clinked their glasses and swallowed.

"Have you ever been in the lighthouse?" Danny asked, eyeing the light tower mischievously.

Emily's eyes followed the tower from its footing to its top, standing at 28 meters tall. Its white bricks glistened in the moonlight to its very top, where its bright beam of light circled endlessly as it had done for nearly 200 yrs.

"No," Emily answered, "to go in you need permission from "Trinity House" and you can only get that if the contractor has the correct qualifications and writes to them or something like that. You need a key code to get in.

"I know, I have the code, unless they've changed it" Danny said, "I had permission before when I worked on the other house" he extended a hand, "Come on, let's go."

"What, right now?"

"It's the perfect time," Danny insisted, "if you think the view is good down here, imagine what it must look like from up there."

Excitedly, Danny led the way to the heavy steel door at the bottom of the tower, the hinges rusted with age, creating a high pitch screeching noise that echoed up the spiralling staircase. At the base of the stairs, Danny flicked a switch, and to their surprise, the staircase became bathed in orange light. Danny led the way, brushing away cobwebs as he ascended the stairs. Emily, despite living in the cottage, felt out of place, like a teenage vandal who had broken into some abandoned building. She felt dizzied by the wine and adrenaline and excitement.

The door to the little staircase that led up to the light itself was locked, but they eventually got to the balcony level, where there was a small room with 2 old chairs and a wooden table. Emily picked up an ornate ashtray, brass and embossed. As she ran her fingers over the worn design, she could scarcely make out the shape of a ship. A wooden box sat on the small table. Emily brushed the dust away, inside of which was a beautifully decorative pipe laid securely against the green felt lining of the little box.

"They used to have to keep these old things manned," Danny said, "all night long they'd be up here."

"Yes, I have read a lot about lighthouses since living in the cottage, this one was automated in the mid 1980s," Emily said.

"My grandfather manned this lighthouse and lived up here, could have been your cottage. I'm not sure, he died before I was born. That could be his pipe?"

. . .

Emily smiled, "you should take it, and do some digging to find out more about the family you had working here. It would be so interesting."

"Maybe I'll do that," Danny had begun fiddling with a small door on the ring of glass that surrounded them. He caught Emily's attention as he let out a small gasp, "Emily, you have to see this."

Emily placed the pipe carefully back in its box and followed Danny's hand gestures beckoning her to the balcony of the lighthouse. At the door she stopped and looked at the metal grating that made the flooring of the balcony. She could see straight through the metal grating to the ground below her, the height nauseating.

"I don't know Danny."

"Come on," Danny teased and began bouncing up and down on the platform, "it's completely secure, I promise."

Danny took Emily's hand firmly in his and guided her outside. She kept her eyes closed tightly, taking in the breeze, which was stronger and colder than it had been on ground level. She stepped slowly on the grating, her right hand in Danny's, her left extended forward, until she could feel the cold touch of the steel handrails.

"Open your eyes," Danny whispered.

Emily did, losing her breath from the shock of seeing the bay from this altitude.

"It's absolutely astonishing," she stuttered.

"It's incredible," Danny agreed.

They stood in silence, watching the sea churning under the moon light, the icy wind chilling every part of them, except their hands, which remained interlaced with one another's, warm against each other. Emily moved closer to Danny, pulling herself into his warmth.

"Thank you," she whispered, "for this."

"I love it up here," he smiled; his eyes locked with hers. On impulse, Danny leaned toward Emily, and suddenly they found their lips locked in a long, deep kiss that sent shudders through Emily's body. "I'm sorry," he whispered.

"Don't be," Emily whispered back, and then laughed, "I'm freezing."

"Me too," Danny nodded, "let's get back."

They moved back into the tower room. As Emily latched the little door against the wind, her eye caught a large box that she hadn't noticed before, tucked away under the little wooden table.

She motioned to the box, "what do you suppose is in there?"

"I suppose there's really only one way to find

out." Danny slid the box out from under the table, the scuffing noise it made against the ground indicating its weight.

The latches on the old trunk flipped down, and Emily watched excitedly as Danny lifted the top.

"Are those books?" Emily exclaimed.

"They certainly seem to be," Danny answered, handing Emily a dust covered, hard bound book.

Emily flipped through the pages, eyeing the scribbling. "They look like journals."

"They must have kept logs," Danny speculated, thumbing through a book of similar scribbling.

"How wild," Emily laughed, "we have to come back up here, when the sun's up, you might learn something about your grandfather."

Danny closed his volume, and placed it back in the box, looking towards Emily, who clutched hers against her chest. He let out a small laugh as he pulled the top closed, and latched the trunk shut again.

"Now you have some light reading before bed," Danny joked.

"Speaking of which, it is getting late," Emily replied apologetically.

Danny nodded his head in agreement, and led Emily down the long, winding staircase to the base of the lighthouse. Inside Emily's cottage, Danny settled on the sofa, while Emily retired to her bedroom, placing the old book neatly on her kitchen table. They both fell asleep with ease.

Danny woke sharply to the sound of a scream, the hairs on his arms stood up, goosebumps formed on the bare skin of his arms and chest. He sat bolt upright in the silence of the cottage, the only sound the dull hum of the television from Emily's room. A few moments passed with the silence undisturbed. Danny tried to close his eyes and return to sleep, but that scream kept playing in his mind, until he finally decided he had to be positive that Emily was alright. Danny walked quietly up the stairs to the doorway of Emily's room, doing his best to stay light-footed, to keep the boards from squeaking and moaning under his weight, afraid he might wake Emily.

"Emily," he whispered lightly, through Emily's slightly open door, "are you ok?"

Danny could hear the squeaking of Emily's bed and the light sound of her footsteps as she approached the doorway.

"I'm sorry," he whispered again, "I thought I might have heard you scream; I didn't mean to wake you."

"No, no," Emily whispered back, her face coming

into view as she pulled the door slightly opened, "you didn't wake me. You probably did hear me. I'm sorry, I just have nightmares sometimes. What time is it anyway?"

Danny squinted at his watch through the darkness, "just after four a.m."

"Oh wow," Emily said, rubbing sleep from her eyes, "I don't guess you'd be interested in some coffee?"

"Black will do just fine," Danny said, his normal volume sounding awkward and slightly hoarse in the early morning quietness.

"I'll be right down", Emily said, turning the light in her room on.

Emily could smell the strong scent of coffee as she came down the stairs, catching the sight of Danny, in his white tee shirt, pouring two cups of coffee: the steam rolling into the cool air. They sat at her kitchen table, nursing their hot coffee, both feeling slightly awkward. Danny was the first to break the silence.

"Do you have nightmares often?" Danny asked, "If you don't mind my prying."

"They are pretty regular lately," Emily answered, "I'm sorry again about waking you."

"It's quite alright," Danny reassured, "I'm a good listener if you want to talk about it."

"Oh, I don't want to bother you with that. I've troubled you plenty enough already."

"It's not a bother at all," Danny's voice sounded comforting, "and I don't mean to be nosey. It's just that, waking up screaming like that, it must have been one nasty dream."

"It was," Emily's voice became heavy, "I've been having them the last few weeks. Pretty regularly. It's always like I'm someone else, and there's always this woman, a beautiful woman, but she's always terrified of me. I saw her again last night. She was shaking. She looked like she had been beaten. The way she looked at me in that nightmare, it was like I was about to do something insidious. I could feel it. That's when I woke up."

"Emily, that sounds absolutely awful," Danny said in a warm voice.

"It is," Emily said, "it really is. I don't know why I keep having them."

"Have you always been prone to nightmares like that?"

"Never," Emily admitted, "it used to be that I almost never had them. Since I've been here, though, I just can't seem to shake them."

"At least it was just a nightmare," Danny smiled weakly, "it's probably just from all the stress of moving. New house, new career, new place entirely. That's a lot of change all at once."

"My daughter always says the same thing," Emily laughed, and changed the subject, "Did I tell you she'll be coming to visit?"

Danny smiled sweetly, "I can't wait to meet her."

CHAPTER
THREE

Emily waited impatiently at the train station watching the passengers unload, scanning for her daughter's familiar face. The relief was even greater than she anticipated when she caught Daisy's beaming smile. *How long has it been?* Emily thought to herself, swearing Daisy had gotten even taller since they'd last seen each other. Daisy weaved her slender body through the crowd of strangers.

"Mum!", she exclaimed, reaching Emily with a long embrace, "oh it feels like it's been ages!"

"Well, it has," Emily smiled, kissing her on the cheek, "I'm so glad you've finally made it. I have so much to show you, and you must have so much to share with me. Come on now, let's go get some lunch."

"That sounds lovely," Daisy replied.

Emily took Daisy to a small tavern, perched on the coastline of the Irish Sea. She knew it was exactly the type of place her daughter would love, and a perfect way to welcome her to Anglesey. The place was quaint, with rustic, dark-stained wooden beams and antique nautical themed décor. They took seats by a window overlooking the bay where a mid-afternoon calm seemed to fall over the glass-still water.

"Mum, this place is beautiful."

"Isn't it though?" Emily smiled.

"I always thought we never visited the coast enough," Daisy laughed, "I can't believe you live here now."

"Neither can I," Emily's eye's widened in agreement, "I love it."

Emily allowed Daisy a moment to take in the view, before placing her hands on top of hers, "now, tell me everything. How are you liking university?"

"It's still as amazing as it was when you asked me on the phone two days ago," Daisy laughed deeply.

Emily was glad that she had still retained some of her teenage sarcasm; that her daughter hadn't yet been completely surrendered to adulthood.

"Well," Emily chuckled, "have you met any cute college boys yet?"

"Mum," Daisy blushed, "no. How about you? Met any ruggedly handsome fisherman here on the coast?"

"Actually," Emily pondered how to best articulate her answer, "I know this is going to sound strange for you, but I want to be honest with you. There is a man here in town that I've kind of started seeing."

Daisy's smile grew wide, "why would that be strange for me?"

"Your dad and I have been together for nearly your entire life. I just figured the idea of me dating would," Emily paused, "I don't know, make you uncomfortable."

"Mum don't be ridiculous. You're a single, grown woman. I want you to date, to be happy. I want the same for dad. I'm not a child, I understand that you two had to go your separate ways. Part of that is inevitably moving on. I just can't believe you haven't mentioned it. Now, tell me everything. Is he cute?"

Emily breathed a sigh of relief, "I can't believe what a mature young woman my little girl has grown up to be."

Daisy's mouth formed a crooked grin, "yes, yes. Now go on, is he cute?"

"He's incredibly handsome, and such a kind man. He's the one who has been working on all the repairs at the cottage. That's how we met."

"Well, when am I going to meet this handsome handyman?"

"Would you really like to?" Emily's face formed a surprised expression.

Daisy sharpened her eyes at her mother, challenging her need to even have posed the question.

"Alright," Emily continued, "how about dinner tomorrow?"

"I'm looking forward to it," Daisy slyly smiled, "now let's eat, I'm dying to see your coffee shop and this wretched cottage that needs so many," Daisy formed air quotes around the final word, "repairs." They both began laughing hysterically.

Emily and Daisy finished their lunch with light conversation. Daisy talked about her lecturers and her friends, those she liked and those she wasn't overly fond of, lodged a litany of complaints about her roommates, and lamented about the awful food on campus. Emily listened intently, offering any advice she could, and shared a list of things she couldn't wait to show Daisy; beaches, the uniquities that could be found at some of the small local shops.

"It's getting pretty late," Emily finally interrupted their catching up, "how about I take you home and get you settled in? You can come with me in the morning to see the shop, sound good?"

"That sounds delightful."

Emily paid the tab and the two of them made the short drive to Emily's home.

"Wow," Daisy commented as the car approached the little row of cottages, "this is even more beautiful than you described. Which one is ours?"

"The one on the very end," Emily pointed, "at the base of the lighthouse."

"Do you own the lighthouse too?" Daisy's voice boasted excitement.

"I wish," Emily laughed, "I can, however, take you to the top of it tomorrow if you'd like."

"How amazing," Daisy exited the car as quickly as it was parked, running to the furthest point of the cliff, calling back, "this is so incredible!"

Emily's entire being warmed with the confirmation that Daisy liked her new home. Hers was the only approval that mattered, and now, she had it.

Emily allowed Daisy some time to appreciate the landscape of her little property before taking her inside the cottage, where a brief tour ended in the spare of the two bedrooms, modestly furnished and cleaned perfectly spotless.

"It's not much," Emily said.

"This is perfect."

"Well, why don't you get unpacked and settled in. I'll go get a couple of glasses of wine poured for us."

"That sounds great," Daisy replied with a smile, "I'll be down in a bit."

Daisy took in every rustic little detail, breathing in the sweet smell of furniture polish. She placed her bags on the bed and removed her shoes, the hardwood floors warm against her bare feet in the little square formed from the late-afternoon sunlight pouring in through the small window. Through the little window, Daisy could see the white bricks of the lighthouse tower and, if she crouched low enough, she could see to the very top, catching the slightest glimpse of the circular, glass encased room.

"Beautiful," she whispered to herself, and began unpacking her things.

. . .

"Daisy, Daisy come to me" a low male voice called to her.

"Hello" Daisy called out, "Mum" who's here?

Emily called up and said "No one here darling, you ok"

"Oh yes, thought I heard someone call me" *must have been hearing the TV* she thought.

Daisy finished unpacking and joined her mum on the sofa for a glass of wine.

They talked, reminiscing about Daisy's childhood, speculating about the future, and making plans for all the things they would do while she visited, long after the sun had set, enveloping the little cottage in the quiet blanket of night. Emily had just reminded Daisy of some embarrassing moment or another from when she was little, which left them both laughing to the point of tears, when a loud thud echoed from upstairs, startling them both.

"What was that?" Daisy asked, the laughter coming to an abrupt stop.

"I'm not entirely sure," Emily admitted.

They sat quietly for a few moments in anticipation.

"Must have been— ", Emily began to speak when, suddenly, another noise sounded from the upstairs as if someone had dropped a heavy object on the floor. They both jumped.

"What the hell" Emily muttered to herself, rising from the couch, "I'll be right back."

Daisy followed behind her mum as she ascended the steps. Halfway to the second floor, she stopped dead when the sound much like that of a chair being dragged across the floor sounded, close to them, as if in the little hallway right at the top of the steps.

"Mum," Daisy asked, frozen in place as Emily continued her way up, "should we call someone?"

"I'm sure it's nothing," Emily assured, forcing a certainty in her voice, as she disappeared at the crest of the stairway.

Daisy remained on the stairs, nervously listening to the sound of boards creaking under her mother's steps, preparing herself for another unexpected noise.

"I don't see anything," Emily called out moments later, "maybe there's a squirrel or something in the attic. I'll have Danny look in the morning."

Daisy breathed a sigh of relief, and followed her mother upstairs, having a look around the hallway and two small bedrooms herself. Standing in Emily's room, they exchanged glances, and Emily shrugged, and opened her mouth to speak. Before she could get any words out, the unmistakable sound of a door slamming shut boomed up the stairs, sounding as if it came from the front door, which was situated just at the bottom of the stairway. Daisy let out a small shriek, while Emily, trying to remain brave for her daughter, walked to the top of the stairs, and glanced down at the front door, which remained closed, and as Emily could see from this vantage point, locked as well.

"Mum," Daisy asked, clearly shaken, "that sounded like a door being slammed shut. Maybe we should call the police or something."

"Don't be ridiculous," Emily insisted, "I'm sure it was just the wind blowing one of the shutters about or something like that? Come on, we'll go have a look."

Daisy kept her phone in her hand, unlocked and ready to use, as she hesitantly followed her mum throughout the house, ensuring that all the windows were securely closed and locked. Emily opened the front door, and a cool breeze washed over them

"See," Emily said with a laugh, "it's just the wind knocking something about. It's an old house. Old houses make noise." She shut the door and bolted it closed.

Daisy remained, shaken and nervous as they resumed their position in the little sitting room area, and continued to enjoy their wine and conversation, a welcome distraction that eased them both. Their conversation continued, undisturbed, well into the night. Exhausted, they finally retired to their rooms for the evening, both ready to welcome a night's rest. The moon hung high in the sky, casting a bright light into Daisy's room. At the window, she took one last glance up at the old lighthouse tower, its huge beam cutting through the sky like a blade. Daisy felt an unexplained feeling of uneasiness as she slid the window open, pulling the shutters in tight, and ensuring the window was locked shut. In the darkness, Daisy drifted to sleep to the sound of the faint humming from her mum's television.

Daisy woke abruptly to the loud clapping sound of the shutters as they slapped against the side of the cottage. Fighting against the daze of her slumber,

Daisy was still processing the noise that had just pulled her from her sleep, when a stroke of light illuminated the little room, quick as a camera flash, before she was cast back into near pitch darkness. Daisy was left speechless, now fully awake and dumbfounded. Her mind raced at a pace equivalent to her heart as she tried to gather what had happened, but she only had a moment before the light once again brushed through the room, the contrast against the total darkness that existed only moments before burning her eyes. She closed them tight and buried her head under the covers. *It's nothing to worry about* she tried to convince herself, but the strong, burning smell of smoke forced her to pull back the covers, just as the light flashed back into her room. In the sliver of time that the space remained illuminated, she saw the unmistakable shape of a man standing at the foot of her bed, unleashing a blood-curdling scream that pulled Emily from her sleep, sending her sprinting to Daisy's room.

Emily threw the door open and turned the lights on, arriving even before the flash of light could return. There was nothing.

"What is it," Emily asked, panting and half awake, "what's wrong?"

"The--," Daisy stuttered behind tears and heavy breathing, "there was a man!"

"A man?" Emily asked, confused, "where?"

"There," Daisy managed, pointing toward the foot of her bed, "right there!"

Emily glanced her eyes quickly around the little room, "Daisy, there's no one here."

"There was!" Daisy insisted, "and there was a bright light that kept turning on, and then off again!"

Emily sat on the bed and placed her hand on Daisy's forehead, wiping back the sweat, "there's no one here Daisy, you must have had a nightmare."

"It wasn't a nightmare," Daisy pleaded, "it was real. I saw him. He was tall and had a beard and he reeked of smoke."

"I know how real nightmares can seem sometimes," Emily said in a calm, motherly voice, "you know that. It's like you can't even tell that you were asleep."

"I'm not a bloody child, mum. I know it wasn't a nightmare."

"OK, ok calm down a moment, he's not here now obviously, so where did he go?

"I don't know," Daisy said forcefully, frustrated, "but he was here!"

Emily stood, stooping below to look under the bed, and walked over to the little window, pulling hard in a display to show that it was locked, "well, he's not under your bed, and he couldn't have gone through the window. Let's go check the rest of the house."

Daisy followed reluctantly. The two went together, checking the locks on the front door, and meticulously checked that every window in the house was locked, and inspected every closet at Emily's insistence; like a mother trying to prove to her child that there wasn't a monster, "see, there's no man here. Nothing more than a nightmare."

Daisy said nothing.

"Anyway," Emily continued, "I have to open the café in a few hours. What do you say we head on over there; I can make you some coffee and breakfast before we open."

"Fine," Daisy stated sternly, still aggravated by her mom's disbelief.

Daisy returned to her room, stopping in the doorway; nervous to enter. She swallowed her nerves, and made haste entering the room, getting dressed as quickly as her body would move. In the process, she placed her foot on something wet near the foot of her bed. Investigating, she found two small puddles, about a shoulder's width apart.

"Just some leaky pipes in the attic, I'm sure," her mother replied when shown the water. Daisy finished getting dressed downstairs.

Sitting at the dining room table, waiting for her mother, Daisy noticed an antique-looking book, and began to thumb through it. The pages of the book were handwritten, mostly dates and notes about the weather, the conditions of the sea, and indecipherable notes about the operation of the lighting mechanism. *Definitely old*, Daisy thought to herself, observing the dates, *this log must have been from the year nineteen twenty*. Nearing around halfway through the book, a small photograph fell onto the table. In the photograph, there was a man, who appeared aged in a handsome way. His face was serious in its expression, his eyes seemingly hollow. The man's arm was draped around a woman, pretty and much younger in appearance than the man. On the back of the picture, the names Blake and Agnes were scribbled. Daisy studied the bearded face of the man obsessively. She was certain; it was the same man she had seen standing at the foot of her bed.

"Mum," She called loudly, "come here!"

"What is it?" Emily asked, slipping an earring in as she walked into the kitchen.

"Look at this photograph, this is the man that I saw, I swear it."

Emily studied the photograph momentarily, a sickened look washing over her face.

"What is it?" Daisy asked, noticing the change in expression.

"That's," Emily stuttered, "that's the woman I've been seeing in my dream. Where did you get this?"

"It fell out of this," Daisy held the old logbook up, "you're positive that this is the woman you've been seeing in your dreams?"

"I wish I could say no," Emily's voice was defeated, "but I've seen her so much, I couldn't mistake that face."

"Who are they?"

"I don't have the slightest idea."

"You're sure. I mean, really sure, that you've seen this woman," Daisy held the picture up again, "in the nightmares that you've been having? Maybe it's just a woman who looks similar?"

"It's her," Emily could hardly stand to look at the photograph.

"This is the man I saw in my room Mum," Daisy

asked, her voice shaky and tears forming in her eyes, "can we please leave?"

Emily nodded her head in agreement, and the two hurried out of the house. The car ride to the café was mostly quiet. Neither wanted to discuss the realization that had just occurred, or speculate the reasoning or significance, but there wasn't a distraction big enough to pull their minds away from it.

"Mum," Daisy was the first to break the silence, "there's something going on at that cottage. I mean, think about it. You've been seeing some woman in your nightmares for weeks and then all of a sudden, I see some man last night? And they both show up in an old photograph, together, from a hundred years ago?"

"Listen to us," Emily said unsteadily, shaking her head and handing the photograph back to Daisy, "we must sound like absolute loons."

"I don't think we should go back," Daisy insisted.

"Let's just get through the day," Emily said, trying to sound happy, "let's just get it out of our heads for a little while and we'll figure it out. We can always get a room if we need to."

Daisy nodded in agreement as Emily parked behind the little café. She unlocked the back door as she always did, and quickly flicked the lights on. They both looked around the little coffee shop wearily, suspicious and still shaken.

"Mum, this place looks amazing, the photos you sent don't do it justice."

"Thanks," Emily smiled, glad to have their conversation on a new topic, "let me get us some coffee going, we could both use it."

As Emily and Daisy finished their coffee, and the breakfast that Emily had made, Shelly arrived promptly on time to help open the shop.

"Good morning, Shelly," Emily greeted as she let Shelly in.

"Morning, Boss," Shelly said, cheerful and full of energy as always.

"This is my daughter, Daisy. Daisy, this is Shelly, she helps me keep this place running."

"It's great to meet you," Shelly said excitedly, "I've heard lots about you."

"All good I hope," Daisy blushed.

"Why don't you guys sit and chat a bit," Emily insisted, "I'll get us ready to open."

"Get paid to chat?" Shelly laughed, pouring more coffee for her and Daisy, "You don't have to ask me twice." Daisy and Shelly sat together at a small table at the back of the shop, while Emily busily set to preparing the café to open.

"So," Shelly smiled, "how do you like it here so far?"

"Oh, it's just beautiful," Daisy beamed.

"Bit different than London, eh?"

"Quite a bit," Daisy chuckled, "but in a good way."

"How do you like the little lighthouse cottage?"

"It's," Daisy fumbled for the words, "it's really great."

"Even better now that Danny is getting some of the issues fixed for Mum." Daisy smiled,

"Have you met Danny yet?" Shelly grinned.

"No, not yet, but we're meeting him for dinner tonight. I've heard a lot about him though."

"You'll love him," Shelly beamed, "he's a really nice guy."

When Emily went out the back of the shop and out of hearing distance, Daisy blurted out "There is something really odd about the cottage, its haunted, I think."

Shelly, paused before speaking, "I have been telling your mum about the stories that surround the Lighthouse, but I was half joking. What do you mean by haunted?"

"I saw a man in my room last night, this morning, I found this photo, and this is him.

"Oh," Shelly exclaimed, you have seen the light housekeeper, he's in the legends"

"What legends?" Daisy asked.

"Oh, just stories," Shelly replied,

"What kind of stories?" Daisy insisted.

"Oh, all kinds," Shelly laughed, "murder, affairs, suicides."

"Are any of them true?"

"I don't know," Shelly shrugged, "I suppose it's hard to know what's true and what's not when it comes to those sorts of stories, but there have been rumors of the light house and the cottages being haunted for years, passed down the generations, that my grandfather told. Apparently, there was a murder there over a hundred years back. We thought the stories were to frighten kids away from there as it's so dangerous on those cliffs.

"It was probably just a nightmare," Daisy replied, doubt in her voice, "but I swear I woke up to the lighthouse beam flashing in my room and I saw a man standing at the foot of my bed in the light, but as soon as my mum came in, he was gone."

"And he looked like the man in the photo?" Shelly asked.

THE LIGHTHOUSE

"Yes, just like the man in this photograph."

Shelly's eyes moved back and forth between Daisy and the photograph, "that's so bizarre."

"It gets even stranger," Daisy whispered, and watched as Shelly's eyes became fixated on her, "my mum's been having these nightmares about a woman, and she swears that the woman she sees in them is the same woman as in this photograph."

"That's too weird," Shelly's voice became serious, "actually, one of the local stories I remember hearing when I was a kid was about a man named Blake."

"Are you serious? What's the story?"

"The story goes," Shelly started, "that Blake was the lighthouse keeper, back in the 1800s. He was a total control freak, a real arsehole, and then one day he snapped, and murdered everyone else that lived there."

"You think that's true?"

"Honestly," Shelly laughed, recognizing how pale Daisy had become, "it's local legend, you never know what's true and what's not."

"Yeah, I suppose you're right," Daisy forced a small laugh.

"You could always find out I guess," Shelly stated coolly.

"What do you mean?" Daisy asked curiously.

"Dig into the history of the place, you know? Look at some old archives, newspapers, things like that. See what you find."

"Oh," Daisy chuckled, "I wouldn't even know how to start."

"Well, you have a picture, with two names, which is a good start. I have just finished a history degree, so I've actually done stuff like this quite a bit. I'm pretty good at putting pieces of the past together. I would totally help you if you wanted."

"Really?"

Shelly nodded her head proudly.

"I don't want to waste your time," Daisy responded.

"You wouldn't be wasting my time at all," Shelly insisted cheerfully, "I love this sort of stuff. I just need to convince your mum to let me have the day off, which I'm sure she will if she knows what we're doing."

"Actually, I don't think we should tell her. Not just yet. She's been really stressed, and I don't want to make it worse for her. If we find anything, then I can tell her."

"I get that," Shelly smiled, "that's sweet of you.

Let me go chat with her, I'll think of something," Shelly winked as she left the table.

A few moments later, Shelly returned to the table with a big smile, holding both of her thumbs upright. Convincing Emily to allow her to have the day to show her daughter around was an easy feat for Shelly.

"Be careful," Emily said to both girls as they were leaving, "and don't forget Daisy, make sure you're back in time for dinner tonight."

"Yes, mum," Daisy called back, and left with Shelly, feeling mix of excitement, nerves, and curiosity.

A few quick searches on the internet didn't reveal much in the way of information about the lighthouse, or its previous owners, so Shelly and Daisy started with what they thought would be the most obvious next choice; the local record office. Here, Shelly's experience navigating old archives helped them to establish at least a faint idea of the history of the little lighthouse. The lighthouse itself bore little information of interest for the two; it was built in 1809 and remained manned until 1980 when Trinity House changed it to an automated system. They had maintained ownership of the property, retaining the light tower itself, but selling off the cottages. Beyond learning that Shelly wasn't exaggerating about how many times the cottages had changed hands over the few decades since being sold to private owners, the old property records didn't bear much in the way of information about the cottage's past inhabitants.

"Now what," Daisy asked, sounding defeated.

Shelly pondered for a few moments, finally exclaiming, "I got it!"

"What?"

"I can't believe I didn't think of it before," Shelly was excited, and hurried to gather her things, "come on, come on, we don't have all day," she laughed.

Daisy followed suit, gathering her things and trailing Shelly to her car, "where are we going?"

"My house," Shelly boasted, her neon pink hair bobbing as she sped down the small streets, "I have access to a ton of online newspaper archives. I mean archives that date back as far the eighteen hundreds. We'll definitely find something."

"I didn't even know there were such things," Daisy gleamed, excited about the prospect.

"Oh, it'll blow your mind," Shelly laughed.

The drive to Shelly's little apartment was quick, and it bore every telltale sign of a history fanatic, with books and papers scattered about, each seemingly about a different significant moment in history. In the corner, Shelly quickly booted her computer and logged onto an archive website.

"Full access," Shelly chuckled, "now, how do you think we should start?"

"How about," Daisy eyed the search bar, "Blake and Agnes?"

Shelly quickly typed and slammed the enter bar enthusiastically; the archive populated some few thousand responses. Shelly scrolled through the first few results and quickly realised that they would need to be more specific.

"How about," Shelly said aloud, and she began typing in the search bar, "Blake, Agnes, Lighthouse, and Anglesey," she pressed enter.

They waited for the website to populate the results, this time a much more manageable number; only a few hundred. Shelly and Daisy's eyes stayed glued to the small snippets of articles and headlines as they scrolled through the search results.

"Bingo!" Shelly shouted, pointing to an article which showed a thumbnail of the familiar row of cottages, and read the headline out loud, "Lighthouse Claims Another Victim: Keeper Blake Conaway Dead."

"Wow," Daisy exclaimed, "open it up."

They opened the article and gasped in unison as it loaded, bearing pictures of individuals, two of which were hauntingly familiar. Emily held the small photograph against the screen, "yep, that's definitely them."

Shelly, shaking her head in disbelief, began reading the article out lout, "Local lighthouse keeper Blake Conaway has allegedly committed suicide following the untimely death of his best friend, Jack Lawson, and the mysterious disappearance of his loving wife, Agnes Conaway. Fellow lighthouse keeper, Benjamin Campbell, says that the loss must have been too much for Mr. Conaway to bear, resulting in the taking of his own life."

"Woah," Daisy interrupted, "that's the man I saw without a doubt."

"Wait," Shelly boomed, "listen to this. Much like the recent disappearance of Mrs. Conaway, the death of Lawson remains veiled in a mist of unanswered questions and unexplained circumstances. With the death of Conaway marking the third life to be claimed on the grounds in the recent weeks, local law enforcement remains of the opinion that the deaths have been of mere misfortune and suspect that Mrs. Conaway likely suffered a similar accident as Lawson, though her body remains yet to be discovered. In the wake of so much tragedy, one can't help but speculate of malevolence."

"Are there any other articles?" Daisy asked.

Shelly printed out the article and went back to the search results, where the two continued to peruse the various headlines and descriptions. There were a few similar to the first, some even more sensational, but none that provided much more information beyond what they had already attained, which was still vague at best.

"Look at that one," Daisy said, pointing. Shelly opened the article.

The article was titled, "Mystery of Agnes Conaway Still Unsolved." The article was short, and definitely not headline news, but it detailed the story of Agnes's parents and their financial troubles, outlining how her mother and father could not find closure as they couldn't find their missing daughter Agnes.

"That's so sad," Daisy commented.

"Look at the date, nineteen thirty-four. That's ten years after this article was written," Shelly said, holding up the printed version of the first article and shaking her head, "ten years and they still hadn't found a body."

"Could you imagine?" Daisy asked inquisitively,

"there can't be anything worse than not having some kind of closure. To have your daughter just vanish into thin air like that."

Shelly turned off her computer, "For two people to die like that, so close together, and for another one to completely vanish, you have to wonder what really happened up there."

"It's a shame," Daisy said wearily, "I guess we'll never know."

"Well, I have another idea," Shelly said gleefully, "but you have to be open-minded."

"I'm all ears," Daisy said curiously.

"We should head to your mum's; I think she should hear this too."

CHAPTER

FOUR

It was 1921, Blake had been working at the lighthouse, perched on the Northern tip of the Isle of Anglesey, overlooking the Irish Sea, since 1909. The lighthouse was already nearing antiquity when Blake had first begun working there. It was built in 1809 and in the decades since, lighthouse technology had been improving at a feverish pace, some even rumoured to be using electric lamps and automated rotating mechanisms. The lighthouse where Blake worked still ran on an oil vapour lamp, rotating with mechanisms that required constant setting and resetting to keep the lamp turning. Even then, the beacon of the lighthouse shone for over twenty miles off the north coast of Anglesey, allowing ships to seek harbour from the cruel vengeance of the Irish Sea in foul weather and negotiate the harsh rocks off the coast of Anglesey.

The lighthouse sat on a rocky outcrop, overlooking the Irish sea over the high, sheer cliffs that surrounded it. The lighthouse remained isolated, the closest village being an inconvenient, almost four-mile journey, not easily navigated by any means, and scarcely suitable for the relatively new automotive technology. Blake, inclined to be social, frequently contended with the walk into the small village on a regular basis, whenever he was off duty, frequenting the small taverns along the old, cobbled streets, and drinking heavily into the night with the other patrons. It was on one of these trips that he first spotted Agnes.

Blake was immediately taken aback by her sight; young and petit, with a still child-like figure. Her long, dark hair flowed like a waterfall down her back, nearly to her waistline. Her eyes were brown, like an aged bourbon, and equally as intoxicating. In the weeks that followed, Blake would find her as frequently as he could, eavesdropping on her conversations, and paying her an occasional slight smile. He admired her intelligence, and how well articulated she was. What he liked even more, at least at first, was how the compliments that he paid her, and the charming advances that he made, seemed to have no effect on her; not like it did on the other women. It was a chase, for Blake, and for the first few months, he relished every minute of it. Agnes, however, had no intention of falling for Blake's charm, and was aware of his reputation for drinking, and for womanising. When the thrill of the heavy flirting, and what Blake perceived as Agnes playing hard to get, wore off, Blake's chasing began to morph. It became a goal, like Agnes was a trophy he intended to win, and when he overheard a conversation between Agnes' parents, John and Mary, he saw an opportunity.

"We don't have a choice," John had said, hammering a for sale sign into the ground in front of the little ale house and Inn their family had owned for generations.

"Because of you," Mary scoffed in disgust.

"I've bloody apologised," John snapped back, "more than enough. It was a mistake."

"It wasn't a mistake," Mary's tone rose, "All of your gambling and now look what it's cost us. It's taken everything."

John shook his head and drove the sign the

remainder of the way into the ground as Mary walked away.

Blake called out to John, who eyed him suspiciously.

"If you're with Jackson, tell him I'm working on getting his money. He can stop sending you people to intimidate me," He demanded immediately.

"I'm not sure of who this Jackson is," Blake insisted, "and I'm not here to intimidate. It's just that I overheard you and your wife, and I think I can help."

"Why don't you just mind your bloody business," John snapped back, and began to walk away.

"If it's money you need," Blake called out, "I have plenty of it."

John stopped and turned his gaze to Blake, desperate and intrigued by the mention of money.

"Let's get a drink and I will explain," Blake smiled, and John nodded his head in agreement, following Blake into the ale house. The two took a seat at a table, in the corner of the dimly lit bar, out of earshot of any curious ears.

"So," Blake started, "how much do you need?"

"I owe a man several hundred pounds," John replied, hanging his head.

"Give me an exact number," Blake insisted, "and I'll give it to you."

"You don't even know me," John replied, "why would you want to help me?"

"You're right," Blake admitted, "I don't know you, but I do know your daughter."

"Agnes?" John asked, surprised.

"Yes, Agnes," Blake confirmed.

"What about her?"

"I want her hand in marriage," Blake smiled.

John couldn't think of how to respond. Blake allowed him a few moments of silence, before he started again, "it's simple. You give me your daughter's hand, and I'll give you more than enough money to pay your debt to this Jackson fellow. Maybe you won't even have to sell your business. She'll have a good life. I work at the lighthouse, the one on the northern shore. I'm the head keeper now."

"I don't know," John responded, shaking his head.

"What other choice do you have?" Blake challenged, "is selling this even going to cover the debt? Besides, what are you going to do after you sell it? Find a job at your age? You'll be broke. You'll live out the rest of your years in destitute. Hell, who knows if your wife will even stick around. And –."

"That's enough," John interrupted, slamming his fist on the table, "I'll do it. I'll talk to Agnes tonight, and she'll be yours to marry."

"Smart man," Blake smiled slyly, "smart man."

The two shook hands, and Blake bought a drink for John, leaving him several pounds as a gesture of good faith.

"I'll return to town the day after next," Blake said, "with your money, and the expectation of it being the day I get engaged to your daughter.

John nodded his head, and Blake disappeared into darkening evening streets. John finished his ale, keeping his head dropped the entire return to his home, dreading the news that he was about to deliver. When he arrived at his little house, Agnes was singing in the kitchen, some joyful tune, while helping her mother prepare dinner.

"Hey daddy," Agnes called out with a smile, seeing John hang his coat on the rack by the door.

"Hey sweety," John replied glumly.

"What's wrong?" Agnes asked.

"He's upset because he's bloody lost all our money gambling. He put the ale house up for sale today."

"What?" Agnes asked, her eyes growing wide, "the ale house is everything to you."

"Gambling is everything to him," Mary chimed in sarcastically.

"That's enough," John said, raising his hand, "we might not have to sell the place after all."

"How can that be?" Mary challenged, "where else are you going to come up with the money to pay for these debts?"

"A man came to me today," he responded, "he's willing to give us more than enough money to pay the debts."

"Well, that's great news?" Agnes asked sweetly, still bewildered by the entire situation.

"Well, what does he want?" Mary asked, "no man is just going to give you that kind of money for nothing."

John paused, deliberating how to deliver the news of what the man's request was. After a few moments, he just spoke the words, that would be a devastating blow to his daughter. "He has an interest in taking Agnes' hand in marriage."

"What," Mary exclaimed, "who is he? Is he a good man?"

"His name is Blake," John responded, "he seems like a fine man. He works out at the lighthouse. He's just been promoted to head keeper there. He makes a good living."

"No, no, no," Agnes shouted, breaking from being dumbfounded by the idea of being married off, "I know that man. I won't marry him."

"Why not?" Mary asked.

"Because, mother," Agnes pleaded, "the man is womanizer and a drunk. Everyone knows that."

"Agnes," John said apologetically, "maybe he's not the man you always wanted to marry, but he seems like a fine fellow. He can provide you a good life."

"No," she insisted, "I won't."

"Agnes," her father started, but Agnes sprinted up the steps and into her bedroom, slamming the door behind her. Her father stood, defeated and emptied, full only of the guilt for the situation he had created.

"She'll come around," Mary said, "she's plenty old enough to be a wife, and if this Blake is a good man, then she will marry him."

John shook his head and remained silent, retiring to his own bedroom. John remained the rest of that night in his room, sulking, racking his brain for any other way that he might come up with the money. He loved his daughter more than anything, the way only a father could, and the guilt of marrying her off to someone she didn't love sickened him. He fell asleep, his eyes red and raw from the tears. Just as dawn broke, and the first small rays of sunlight creeped through the little window in his room, landing in perfect little streaks on the floor, he woke to a light knocking on the door.

"Daddy," he heard Agnes whisper, "are you awake?"

"Yes," John called back, his old bed creaking under his weight as he rose, letting Agnes in.

"If it gets you out of this debt, then I'll do it."

"Agnes," he said, placing his arm on her shoulder, "I've thought about it too, and I wouldn't feel right doing that to you."

"I'm going to do it," Agnes replied, her eyes teary, "and you can't talk me out of it. But promise me that you're done gambling."

"Are you sure?"

"Promise me that you're done," Agnes said, tears now running down her cheeks.

"I am," John said, his own tears beginning to pool in his eyes, "never again, I swear."

Mary was ecstatic to hear that Agnes had agreed and set to work getting things in order for when Blake would return. The next morning, it was Agnes that heard the knocking on the door, and opened it to see Blake, cleaned up and well dressed.

"Hi, Agnes," he said sweetly.

"Good morning," she responded.

"Listen," Blake started, dropping to his knees, "I know that I might not be the man of your dreams, and that you've likely always imagined someone else as your husband. But I'm going to do everything I can to make you happy, you have my word. I'll do anything that you ask me to, and anything that I don't know how to do, I promise that I'll learn," he paused, slipping a pretty little ring onto her slim finger, "from this point on, you are my universe, the very air that I breath, the water that I drink, the food I consume. You are everything."

Tears of joy rolled down Agnes' face, unprepared for Blake to make any type of gesture, and certainly not expecting the lovely words that poured from his mouth. Blake stood and pulled Agnes in for a tight embrace. John and Mary walked into the room, not being able to help smile at seeing the way that Blake held their daughter.

"Well," John interrupted, extending a hand to Blake with the look of a fool painted on his face, "welcome to the family I suppose."

Blake smiled and shook John's hand in a vice

tight grip, and then introduced himself to Mary, who found his charm and wit to be undeniably attractive, and, after learning of his career at the lighthouse, she was certain that he was more than capable of making her young daughter a happy wife. Mary always imagined an elaborate, beautiful wedding for her only child, but given how rapid the union was to happen, and their lowly financial state, a modest ceremony was held, attended only by a handful of John, Mary, and Agnes' family and close friends. Blake had no relatives, no friends or acquaintances, who made an appearance. The two were wed in the local chapel.

The next morning, Blake helped Agnes pack her meager belongings, and she left with him, as a new wife, to the small cottage he lived in, at the base of the lighthouse where he worked. It was a whirlwind for Agnes, having been married so suddenly, so quickly, and now leaving her childhood home equally as fast. The entire process felt very sterile, efficient, and mechanical. She grinned and bore it the best she could. When the two arrived at what would be her new home, she immediately fell in love with the property, the view of the sea, the impressiveness of the gleaming white brick tower, the coziness of the small cottages. Her favorite part was the view from the gallery, where she could stand on the balcony at the very top of the lighthouse, and see for miles into the Irish sea, watching the ships rock up and down in the motion of the water. It was in the gallery that Agnes met Jack, a tall man with a strong build and long, sandy blonde hair, who was pleasant in his introduction of himself, as well as Ben, a younger, slimmer man with a soft smile and kind, dark eyes.

"Gentlemen," Blake had commanded, "this is Agnes. We've just been married."

"Congratulations," both men said in unison.

"Thank you both," Agnes blushed.

"Alright boy," Blake smiled, "I'm going to need you gentlemen to man the tower tonight. I'm a newlywed, and you know what that means." Blake winked, and both men's cheeks turned a rosy red. Agnes felt sick at the expectation that Blake clearly had. She spent the rest of the day unpacking her few belongings and taking in the new environment. The cottage was small, but it was cozy, and she loved the antique feel of it. Blake, it was evident, did not put cleanliness anywhere near the top of his list of priorities. She quickly settled in, and happily set to cleaning the cottage.

"I guess I'm going to make a wife out of you

faster than I thought," Blake laughed, grabbing at Agnes' rear while she scrubbed the hardened food off the dishes that had been sitting in the sink, likely for days.

"I suppose," she chuckled awkwardly, not knowing how to respond to his off-handed comment.

Blake didn't say much for the remainder of the evening as Agnes finished restoring the little cottage to a livable state. Rather, he sat on the old, small sofa in the main living area, smoking from a pipe, the scent of which filled the cottage with a bitter-sweet aroma. Agnes couldn't decide if she liked the smell.

When the evening drew in Blake told Agnes to go upstairs and wait for him. The first night which was supposed to be a wonderful union of 2 people in love had not been what she expected. He was rough, and treated her more like a tramp from a whore house than his wife.

She was grateful that it was over quickly, and that when it was, he rolled over and was asleep before she caught her breath. For her, it felt as though he was a completely different man to the one who wooed her.

Her first night as wife to Blake, head lighthouse

keeper, was an affirmation of what her life would be like. The magic of new romance came and went before she could even tell it was there, if it ever even came at all. She quickly became Blake's ideal version of a housewife. In the matter of weeks, she would clean, and cook, and tend to his every beck and call. While it wasn't the romantic relationship that she had always dreamed about, she didn't find Blake to be an unkind man, not in those first months, and she began to enjoy the satisfaction she found in making him happy. Even the sex wasn't as awful. She held fast to the idea that, given enough time, she might even be able to learn to love him. In the years that followed, she would learn that she was mistaken.

CHAPTER
FIVE

By 1924, Blake and Agnes had been married for three years, which they had spent living in one of four little cottages attached to the lighthouse where Blake worked as the head lighthouse keeper. The two other workers lived in two of the houses attached to theirs. Jack and Ben spent countless hours in the tower, resetting the mechanisms, watching the coastline, and keeping detailed logs of everything from weather conditions to repairs made to the equipment, which kept a steady beam of bright light rotating a steady revolution every 10 seconds, which could be seen from miles away. Blake and Agnes lived in the little cottage situated right at the base of the tower, with Ben's immediately next in line, followed by Jack's, and the fourth and last cottage remaining unoccupied.

Over the past few months, it had become a regular occurrence to hear Blake shouting at Agnes in a drunken rage. While Ben and Jack had developed a strong friendship with Agnes in their years of working at the lighthouse, they seldom interacted with her when Blake was around. When Blake was in one if his rages, mostly Ben and Jack would let it pass, and kept their involvement to conversations with Agnes while Blake was manning the tower; they knew better than to try and confront the man they worked for, less they wanted to find themselves without a job and a home. But, on a night when Agnes let loose a scream so loud that Jack's hair stood on end, he had no choice but to confront Blake. Jack pulled his hood over his head and stepped into the cool, damp night, the heavy rain falls rhythmically and loud, he knocked his bare knuckles against the icy wooden door of Blake's home. The door opened abruptly.

"What is it?" Blake demanded, "isn't Ben on shift tonight?"

"Yes," Jack confirmed, "Ben is."

"Then what could you possibly need?" Blake interrupted, before Jack could get another word out.

"It's just," Jack paused, "it's just that I heard a scream. I wanted to make sure everything was alright."

"Of course everything's alright," Blake growled.

Blake began to shut the door. Jack planted his foot firmly at the base, stopping the door a few inches shy of closing. He tilted his head, his sandy hair falling over his face. Through the small crack, he could see Agnes sitting on the floor, her head buried in her hands. Blake's eyes glazed over with fury as he pushed harder on the door. Blake's strength wasn't enough to overpower Jack's size. Jack's blue eyes became piercing as he locked them with Blake's.

"Are you sure," Jack asked loudly, his voice steady and firm, "that everything is, ok?" His eyes shifted to Agnes in the background.

"Everything is," Agnes stuttered out from behind her tears.

"Nobody asked you," Blake hissed back at her, and turned his glance back on Jack, "now you. I suggest you mind your own goddamned business. Don't forget who works for who around here."

Blake pulled the door open wide, and Jack caught a glance at Agnes, her face reddened and bruising. Jack pulled his foot out of the way just as

Blake threw the door shut with all the force he could muster, the slam echoed into the night. Jack stood, his face inches from the wooden door, as he listened to the muffled sounds of Blake's uproar stirring back up behind the door, shuddering at the haunting sound of every loud thud and bang. His attention was called away by the rattling sound of footsteps on steel grating; a flashlight beam caught his face, and he squinted against the light, looking towards the top of the tower.

"Everything alright down there?" Ben called down from the steel balcony.

"Just fine," Jack called back with a waving motion, "enjoying your night up there?"

"Oh, it's just lovely mate," Ben called back sarcastically.

"If you need anything you know where to find me," Jack yelled back as he headed back for his little house.

Jack laid and listened deftly for cries and screams, contemplating what he wished he would have done, or what he might do, and drifted asleep to the sound of the heavy rainfall. The remainder of the night slunk by quietly, taking with it the rain. Ben welcomed the sound of heavy footsteps, which echoed up the spiral staircase of the tower; his relief was coming to take over. The door creaked open, giving way to Blake, who arrived with disheveled hair and bloodshot eyes. He stumbled over to a small table and let the weight of his body fall into a small wooden chair. Ben waited anxiously for him to say something. He had been on the bad end of Blake's binges enough to know to keep his mouth shut and wait. Blake slid open a small wooden box, removing a wooden pipe from inside, and began packing the tobacco in silence. Ben watched Blake's beard wriggle and change shape as he struck a match and began the succession of short puffs to get the tobacco burning; the smoke filled the room with a sweet aroma.

"Well get on with it boy," Blake's voice was deep and raspy, "what have you got?"

"Nothing sir," Ben stuttered, "we had some rain last night, but nothing out of the ordinary. Equipment is all operating. I've cleaned the lenses also."

"Good lad, good. We'll make a man out of you yet" Blake chuckled, placing his feet up on the table, "easy mornin' for me then."

"Yes sir," Ben nodded, loathing Blake's comments; though the youngest man at the lighthouse, at twenty-eight, he wasn't a boy anymore.

"Well go on then," Blake barked, pulling his worn beret over his eyes, and waving Ben off.

Ben made haste getting back to his little cottage, his eyes burning from tiredness. He went straight for his small bedroom, where he removed his boots and pulled the heavy wool curtains closed tightly, blocking out the brightness of the morning sun. He laid in the darkness, sleep just beginning to crawl over him, when he was startled by a loud thud from behind the wall, *Agnes must be moving furniture around*, he thought to himself, and prayed she wouldn't be at it all day. No more loud noises followed in the minutes to come, but the faint sound of whimpering kept him from drifting off. He rose, and cupped his ear against the wall, more whimpering.

"Is everything alright over there?" He called out loudly and waited.

He heard shuffling, a thud, a sharp cry. He rushed down the stairs and wasted no time lacing his boots up. At Blake and Agne's cottage, he knocked on the door and waited for an answer. Moments went by without an answer, and so he tried again. Still, no answer. He tried to turn the knob, but found the door was locked. When he heard another sharp cry from behind the door, he went quickly to Jack's cottage, knocking on his door heavily until Jack finally opened it.

"Bloody hell what is it?" Jack asked, groggy from having just been woken.

"I think something's wrong with Agnes," Ben posited impatiently.

"Isn't Blake at the tower?" Jack asked, looking at his watch.

"Yes, he is."

"Well did you let him know?", Jack interrupted.

"No," Ben shook his head, "I think he's still bloody drunk. You know how he gets."

Jack sighed, nodding his head in agreement, "what makes you think somethings the matter anyway?"

"I heard something land on the floor over there. I thought she was just moving furniture or something, but I heard her scream a bit, and I'm positive I can hear her crying over there. I knocked on her door, but she didn't answer. You haven't got a key, have you?"

"I don't," Jack shook his head, "but if you're that concerned, we can get over there via the attic."

"Come on," Jack motioned Ben inside.

Inside, Jack led Ben up to the second floor. At the top of the stairs, a small wooden square rested against the ceiling. Stretched out, and on the tips of his toes, Jack could push the piece of wood up, and slide it over, revealing access to the attic of the cottage.

"The attics are all connected," Jack explained, "you can go up here, and cross straight over to Blake's."

"Ok," Ben nodded.

Jack kneeled, interlacing his fingers tightly to make a sort of step for Ben, "go on then. I'll hoist you up there."

Ben placed a hand on Jack's shoulder to brace himself and stepped into Jack's hands. Jack made easy work of lifting Ben up, who easily pulled his thin body up and through the hole. Once in the attic, he whispered to Jack, "what about you?"

"I'll go out front, just open the door when you get over there."

The attic was dark, he hunched over, Ben carefully began moving through the space. He squinted in the darkness and felt ahead with his feet for the beams that could support his weight. As Ben traversed across into the area above Blake's cottage, he was surprised by the faint glow, which illuminated upwards, forming a square of light against the interior of the roof; the access cover above Blake's cottage was already removed. As he neared closer, he could hear the distinct sounds of a woman crying. Ben poked his head through the cover, and called out in a whisper, "Agnes, are you alright?"

Agnes limped out of her bedroom, and was startled by the sight of Ben's head, protruding from the ceiling.

"Oh my god," She shrieked, "what are you doing up there?"

"I thought I heard a scream earlier and heard you crying. I knocked on the door, but you never answered."

"Oh, it's nothing," Agnes said, as Ben hoisted himself down into the hallway.

"You're limping Agnes. What happened?"

"It's really nothing," Agnes insisted.

Ben eyed her ankle, which had become visibly swollen and bluish in colour, and then returned his eyes to the opened access cover, before noticing a small, wooden stepladder leaning against the wall.

"Bloody hell Agnes," Ben exclaimed, "did you fall out of the attic?"

She remained steadfastly silent, but her eyes gave her away in an instant.

"What were you doing up there?" Ben waited for an answer. Tears began to run down her pale cheeks.

"You can't tell Blake," She whispered.

"Of course," Ben said, placing a firm grip on Agne's shoulder, "I'm going to go let Jack in, ok?"

Agnes nodded. Moments later, Jack and Ben were back upstairs. Ben crouched at Agnes's leg, removing her worn boot to inspect her ankle. The purple bruising matched that on her face. Jack finished sliding the cover for the attic back into place and turned his focus to Agnes.

"You're going to need a doctor," Jack said solemnly.

"No, no. I'll be fine," Agnes contested, wincing as she tried to pull her stockings back over her foot.

"He's right," Ben insisted, "if it's not broken, it's at least badly sprained."

Agnes simply shook her head, "it's really alright. Just please, don't tell Blake."

"How are you going to explain your ankle?" Jack kept his solemn tone.

"I'll tell him I slipped on the stairs. Please, please promise that you won't tell him."

"We won't," Ben's eyes shifted to Jack, who nodded in agreement.

"What were you doing up there anyway?" Jack asked.

"It's just," Agnes stopped, "it's really nothing. I

just have things up there, personal things. You know how Blake gets sometimes. There are certain things I don't want ruined is all. It's stupid."

"We understand," Ben said in the most comforting voice he could muster, "we won't tell him."

"We need a doctor," Jack injected, shaking his head in disgust, infuriated by the entire situation.

"Right," Ben agreed, "I'll take my cycle to town and fetch the doctor."

"Help me get her downstairs first," Jack stated.

Ben and Jack helped Agnes to her feet. Supported on the shoulders of the two men, they carefully traversed down the narrow wooden steps, and helped her rest on the small sofa, elevating her badly bruised foot on a small, darkly stained wooden coffee table. Jack took a position next to Agnes, who, from either the pain, or the stress of the morning, or a combination of the two, now had a steady stream of tears running down her face. Jack gently tucked loose strands of her jet-black hair behind her ears and allowed Agnes to rest her head against his shoulder, a gesture which led Agnes into a complete sob.

"Hurry along," Jack motioned for Ben to go.

Ben hurried out to his bicycle, making a racket

as he took off, pedaling furiously. Blake, who stood on the balcony of the lighthouse, steadily smoking his pipe and drinking whiskey from his worn steel flask, was intrigued by Ben's urgency. Blake remained on the balcony, finishing his pipe, conjuring up a litany of reasons why Ben would have been in such a rush. Prone to suspicion, after half an hour of pondering, Blake was inclined to leave his post and headed down the winding staircase towards his cottage. Jack and Agnes were equally startled by the sudden appearance of Blake. Blake's eyes darted quickly around the room, first seeing Agnes crying on Jack's shoulder, and then her elevated foot; swollen and blue. Jack knew instantly that it wouldn't be Agnes' swollen foot that would be Blake's main concern. Rather, it would be the fact that Jack was there, with Agnes. When it came to Blake's jealous tendencies, he was a far cry from inconspicuous about them. In the case of Agnes, it wasn't jealousy over the fact that the woman he loved might be having an affair with someone else, but rather a loathing at the idea of what he considered his property, becoming someone else's property.

"Blake, Agne's fell," Jack started.

"Get up," Blake demanded, interrupting Jack

before he had time to explain, "and get the fuck out of my house."

"Blake," Agnes cried, "I slipped down the stairs, Jack just…"

"I didn't ask you anything," Blake spat, and returned his attention to Jack, "who do you think you are?"

"Blake," Jack said, struggling to keep his voice calm, "Agnes injured her foot badly. Look at it. Ben is on his way to get the doctor."

"A doctor? For what? Agnes is my wife. Mine. I'll decide if she needs a doctor or not," Blake was in a full rage. He stomped to the sofa, grabbing Agnes by the collar of her coat, "get up, I bet you can walk just fine."

Blake pulled Agnes up by her coat, her weight bearing down on her swollen foot caused her to collapse to the floor, letting out a shriek that chilled Jack's very spine.

"You're faking it you bitch," Blake screamed with an unbridled fury that caught even Jack off guard. He grabbed at Agnes again, the same anger in his tone, "get up!"

"That's enough," Jack demanded, his voice loud and stern.

"What did you say," Blake challenged.

"I said that's enough," he repeated.

Blake approached Jack, his alcohol reddened face only inches from Jack, "I always knew you were a snake," he whispered, "how long have you been fucking my wife?"

"Blake," Jack steadied his voice, "you know I'm engaged. You're just drunk. Why don't you go back up to the tower and sleep it off."

"Sleep it off," Blake scoffed, wrapping his fists around the collar of Jack's shirt, "I could kill you," he whispered, "and nobody would ever know a thing."

"Stop," Agnes cried out, "please stop."

Blake pushed Jack, stumbling backwards, his head turned towards Agnes. Jack gathered himself as quickly as he could, preparing for the brawl that he was certain was about to break out. Just as Blake began to stumble towards Agnes, and Jack readied himself to intercept, the cottage door suddenly opened. Ben walked in with a well-dressed man, donning a stethoscope around his neck and a large black bag in his hand. For a moment, the entire room was silent, until the doctor finally spoke, directing his attention at Agnes, who was still laying on the floor, "you must be Agnes?"

"Yes," Agnes replied, trying to suppress her sniffled crying.

"Thank you for coming," Blake said politely, extending his hand, as if he had become a different person, cool and kind, in the blink of an eye, "she fell down the stairs, I think her ankle is hurt pretty badly."

"Of course, of course," The doctor replied, crouching at Agnes's feet and beginning to examine the swollen ankle, "let's just get you up on this chair and have a look here."

A few moments passed in silence as the doctor gently inspected her ankle, Agnes wincing and whimpering with every slight movement.

"Is this from the fall as well," the doctor inquired, lightly touching the bruising on her face.

"Yes," Agnes said, trying to force a tone of confidence, "I hit one of the steps when I fell."

BLAKE SHOT a glance at Ben and Jack, as if daring them to say something about his behavior, or about how they thought her face had really become so marred.

"And how about your head," the doctor continued, examining Agnes's dark brown eyes, "any headaches or dizziness?"

"No," Agnes replied.

"Well," the doctor spoke kindly, "your ankle is most definitely broken. We'll have to get you into town, and have it set and cast," he directed his attention to Blake, "is there anywhere in town that Agnes could stay for a little while? I'd like to be able to make regular checkups, and it would be much more convenient if she was closer to my surgery."

"My parents live in town," Agnes answered.

"Perfect," the doctor smiles, "I know it's an inconvenience, but perhaps you could lodge with them for a few weeks while you heal up."

"What do you think, Blake?" Agnes asked, like a child.

"I think that's a perfectly well-suited idea," he smiled, "I must get back up the tower, but I'll come see you tonight. I'm sure Jack can relieve me a little bit early."

"Of course," Jack stated, his voice monotone.

Blake leaned in and kissed Agnes on the lips, "I'll see you tonight. Feel better," he said, in his most saintly voice.

"Ok," Agnes said, nodding in agreement as Blake left the cottage.

"Then it's settled," the doctor beamed, "we best get you moving. Would you men mind helping me get Agnes out to my carriage?"

Ben and Jack both agreed, and helped Agnes to her feet as the doctor went to open the carriage door, letting her remain stable against their shoulders. Ben let Jack support her petite frame as he took a heavy wool coat from a hook near the door, helping her slip into it.

"Is there anything you want me to send with you?" Ben asked.

"Actually," Agnes replied, "would you mind terribly if I asked you to grab my slippers from upstairs, they're just at the foot of my bed."

"Not at all," Ben replied, heading up the narrow steps.

With Ben upstairs, Agnes slipped her hand into the pocket of her dress, retrieving

a book: small and bound in worn black leather and wrapped tightly closed by the attached matching lanyard. She thrust the book into Jack's hands.

"Jack," she whispered, "I need you to hide this. Please. I hate to ask, but if Blake ever read this, he would murder me."

Jack only nodded and slipped the little book into his pocket. Agnes began the three-mile journey into town with the doctor alone, and she breathed a sigh of relief. Jack and Ben spent a few minutes talking about the craziness of the morning, before Ben retired to his cottage for some long-needed sleep. In Jack's cottage, he sat at the small kitchen table, and allowed his curiosity to get the better of him as he opened the little black book that Agnes had trusted him with and began reading.

It was another awful day today. Blake and I fought again. I just want children so badly. There is nothing I desire more than to be a mother, to start a family. He insists we must wait until he can get a position at the new lighthouse that's being built, where there are no cliffs and children are allowed to live. I fear it'll be years before it's done. I can't wait. I simply can't. If only he would let me stay in town. He's persistent that I would hate it, him having to work for an entire month to have a month off at home with me and the baby. I know I wouldn't mind it; a month is only a month. Besides, he could make trips into town during his off hours, every day if he wanted. I think he simply doesn't trust me to be without him for that length of time, for any length of time, really. He's certain that I'm bound to have an affair, to be picked up by some other man. There is no convincing him otherwise, it seems. No amount of reassurance of my love would suffice. I know Blake wasn't my first choice for a husband, and our marriage is one of circumstances, rather than real love. All I want now is for us to start our own family, to have a little baby for me to love, who I know would truly love me.

Jack thumbed through the rough-edged pages, realising that the book Agnes had trusted him with was her own personal diary. He continued to roll through the pages until he came to a section absent from writing, and then began flipping slowly backwards until he saw ink; the most recent of her writing, dating only a few days earlier. He shuddered at what he read, as his eyes moved from one side of the page to the other, back and forth feverishly.

My fear is becoming increasingly tremendous. Blake has become ever more unpredictable. Every command I contest, or even show the slightest disinterest in, is met with physical reprimand. I cannot escape his control, less I would wind up murdered. He tells me so and I believe him to be plenty capable. Today, he explained in detail how he could do it, and without anyone so much as suspecting him as a perpetrator. He is the very definition of a monster. He has no remorse when it comes to his assaults, no guilt in the beatings, or the name calling, and certainly none in his acts of forcing himself into me whenever he so pleases. If not for my angel, my saviour, I would undoubtedly claim my own life; for I know no other way in which to shed myself of this horrible burden, of the awful mistake I have made in wedding myself to this man, to this monster. Oh please, God, universe, stars, make this man die.

Jack slammed the book shut, physically sickened by the words, and bound the journal up tightly. He understood, now, why she was so insistent this journal be hidden. If Blake had seen these words, it would spell utter disaster for Agnes. Just as Agnes had done, Jack tucked the journal away in his attic, safely hidden from the eyes of Blake, and prepared himself to take post in the lighthouse, worried he wouldn't have the restraint to not simply kill Blake himself.

CHAPTER
SIX

"I wish you and Ben would stop coming here," Agnes whispered sternly to Jack, "He would fire you, or worse. You know he thinks we're..." she trailed off.

"I know what he thinks. He's passed out drunk in the tower. He doesn't know I'm here" Jack assured, "I just wanted to see how you were doing, that's all."

"I'm doing alright," she replied, forcing a small smile and wriggled her cast foot,

"How is Ben?" she asked with a concerned tone.

"Worried about you Agnes, we both are, of course." Jack replied

"How are the wedding plans coning on" Agnes warmed slightly

"Slowly" Jack laughed "who knew the amount of planning that's needed"

Looking at her cast Agnes said "I'm ready for this thing to come off. It's been a very long couple of weeks. The doctor says he'll be able to take it off in the matter of just a few more weeks."

"That's good news," Jack smiled, "then what?"

"Then I come home, I suppose," Agnes answered.

"You can't be serious," Jack shook his head.

"What else am I going to do Jack?"

"Agnes, Blake isn't going to change. You must do something."

"There's nothing I can do," she insisted, "he'll kill me, Jack. I know he would."

"Just run away, Agnes, go somewhere where he can't find you."

"It's not that simple," she snapped back at him.

"It could be," Jacks voice grew stern and serious, "You could…"

"Stop, Jack," Agnes interrupted, "just stop. I can't just disappear. I just can't. you are my best friend Jack; I can't have anything happen to you. You need to get back before he notices you are gone"

"Agnes…", Jack started.

"Please don't," Agnes insisted, tears beginning to well in her eyes, "Go."

Jack submitted to her orders, shaking his head in frustration as he left of the room. Agnes listened, her cheeks now damp with tears, to Jack leaving. The slam of the front door echoed through her parents' house, leaving behind an uncomfortable silence that fell over the entire house. Agnes lay still with her eyes closed tightly, all her energy being expended to maintain her composure, to keep herself from completely unravelling. Minutes passed like this, still, with her cheeks damp with tears. She rubbed her stomach gently with both hands, whispering out loud, "I'm sorry little one. I'm just so sorry...".

A few weeks later, Agnes returned home. In the weeks that she was gone, Blake's drinking had increased. He was in a state of near perpetual inebriation. She relished the nights when he would go into town and drink himself into oblivion, sometimes not returning home until late into the next day. Agnes did everything she could to tend to the demands of Blake. Her life had become the most intricate, delicate of ballets; anything to avoid setting him off, to avoid triggering a violent rage. Anything Blake asked, she did. "I'm doing it for you," she would whisper to her belly after every particularly exhausting, or otherwise unpleasant, duty she would have to fulfill. It worked- mostly. What anguished Agnes more was the life that was slowly growing inside her. Every day she would stand in front of the mirror, watching her belly swelling ever so slightly. For months, she dreaded the day that she would have no choice but to come clean to Blake, and that day came like a freight train; fast and unexpectedly.

"Getting a little plump aren't we," Blake laughed, you should watch be eating less"

"I'm sorry," she instinctively replied, terror trembling over her body. She breathed deeply and braced herself, "Blake. I'm pregnant."

"You bitch," Blake's voice was steady, the most terrifying calm, as he locked eyes with Agnes.

Just as Agnes opened her mouth to speak, a bright flash whited out her vision. Her face seared. She could barely make out the words screaming from Blake's mouth through the ringing that pierced her ears. She wrapped her arms tightly around her stomach, pulling herself into a fetal position. Another blow landed on her face, this time Blake's hand was clenched in a fist, solid as granite. Agnes pulled herself in as tightly as she could, bracing herself for the next set of blows. Blake paced the room in a stomp.

"I bet it's not even mine, is it?" Agnes could feel the heat of Blake's breath against her cheek, the strong smell of whiskey on his breath. "Is it?" he screamed again.

Agnes couldn't speak. She could feel her lips swelling, her throat dry. She nodded her head.

"You're a lying whore," Blake spat at her, "who's is it? Jacks?"

"No," she managed a whimper, "it's yours. I swear it is."

Agnes could feel the heat of Blake's skin as his open palm landed against the side of her face. She pulled her arms up to try and shield the blows. Blake took her wrists, pinning them down on her sides. His grip on her wrist was so tight, she was certain he could crush the bone if he wanted to, his face only millimeters away from her own.

"You're going to get this taken care of. Do you understand? You're not going to be living by yourself while I'm on this godforsaken cliff working. Whoring around right under my nose the way you do now, I can't even imagine if you were left by yourself. Get rid of it."

"No," she cried, her eyes swelling closed, "please, just stop."

He struck her again, this time with as much might as he could muster. "Get rid of it, or I will," he boomed, just as Agnes blacked out.

Blake cursed under his breath, and continued to berate Agnes, even in her unconscious state. He dressed, and laced his boots up furiously, stopping only to take swigs from his flask. Blake was barely coherent by the time he left his cottage and stumbled up the spiralling staircase to the top of the tower, where Jack had been manning the post. Jack could smell the whiskey from the other side of the room.

"Get out," Blake mumbled.

"Do you want me to go over the logs with you?"

"Get out," Blake repeated with increasing volume and aggression.

"Yes boss," Jack said solemnly, and gathered his things, feeling the burn of Blake's gaze, like a magnifying glass on ants.

Passing by Blake, Jack noticed Blake's knuckles, torn and bloody. After leaving the tower, Jack stopped at Blake's cottage, eyeing the top of the lighthouse to be sure Blake wasn't standing on the balcony. He knocked quietly on the door, whispering

Agnes's name against the hardwood. There was no response. Jack stopped at Ben's cottage, who, sensing Jack's uneasiness, welcomed him in immediately.

"I need your help," Jack insisted, not wasting time on pleasantries.

"What's going on?"

"Blake's drunk."

"What else is new," Ben laughed.

"His knuckles are bloody. I've got a bad feeling. I'm worried about Agnes."

"Should I go to her?" Ben's voice became serious, knowing that if Jack was worried, it was for good reason.

"No, I need you to go up the tower, keep Blake distracted while I check on Agnes."

"But I need to see her," Ben lamented,

"No. He will kill you if he thinks anything is going on. Let me go, I at least have a fiancée, and I will be able to defend myself against him. I am bigger and stronger than he is."

Ben was a slight man, shorter and probably weaker than Blake.

"What am I going to tell him when he asks me why I'm up there?"

"Make something up. Tell him you got your days

shuffled up or something, that you thought you were supposed to be on watch today. Offer to help clean the lenses for a bit or something. You're a smart kid, you'll think of something."

"I don't know, Jack, he's a lunatic when he's drunk," Ben said anxiously.

"This is no time for arguing," Jack spoke with purpose to his voice, "go up there and distract him before he suspects a thing."

"Alright. I'll go up. You keep your ear on the ground though, you hear? And be fast."

"I will," Jack nodded, "thank you."

Ben pulled his tattered, green wool coat on, and made way for the tower. He entered cautiously, Blake immediately growling at his presence, "what the fuck are you doing up here, boy?"

"I'm sorry," Ben managed to stutter, "I thought I was on shift now."

"Well, you're not, you bloody idiot," Blake spat.

"Apologies, boss."

"Well," Blake chuckled, "as long as you're here, why don't you just take my shift?"

Ben's heart raced, certain that this was a mistake. Instead of making sure Blake stayed up here, he was going to be the reason Blake returned to the cottage, right when Jack was sure to be there. Ben glanced at Blake's hands- Jack wasn't exaggerating, his knuckles were noticeably torn up, and his face was red as fire; the kind of colour only made by a mixture of rage and alcohol.

"If it's all the same sir," Ben thought quickly, "I would just as soon like to run into town if I'm off shift. I'd be glad to fetch you a fresh supply of whiskey while I'm there, if you'd fancy."

"Now that, boy," Blake laughed, "is an idea."

"Thank you, sir," Ben breathed a sigh of relief.

"Fill the lamp up before you go."

"Yes sir," Ben set to work pouring the heavy oil into the basin of the lamp, while Blake kicked his feet up on the small table and pulled his cap over his eyes. Ben intentionally filled the lamp slowly, not wanting to shorten the length of time he could be in the observation room before arousing Blake's suspicion.

"No cheap shit, boy," Blake muttered as Ben was pouring.

"Of course not, sir," he replied with a smile.

When he finished, he quietly slunk out of the room, and perched himself at the top of the stairs, just outside of the door to the observation room, where he could listen for Blake's movements. It wasn't long before the nerve-racking silence was replaced by the audible sounds of Blake's loud snoring. *Perfect*, Ben thought to himself, and silently waited.

Jack slipped into his cottage, and quickly moved upstairs, removing the access cover for the attic, and hoisting himself up. In the attic, he slinked quietly over to the access cover for Blake's cottage, removing it ever so carefully and quietly. He poked his head through, and called out in a whisper, "Agnes, is everything alright?"

Jack didn't get a response, but he could hear her cries in the bedroom. He let himself down into the hallway, and knocked gently on Agne's bedroom door, whispering, "Agnes, are you alright?"

"Jack", he heard her whisper, "is that you?"

Jack pushed the door open slowly, revealing Agnes, curled tightly against herself in her bed, the blanket pulled over her still naked body. He teared up at the sight of her face, bruised and bloody, her mouth and eyes so swollen she could hardly open them. He helped her to her feet, Agnes moaning in pain from her sore and stiffened muscles.

"Christ, Agnes," He gasped, "what happened?"

"I'm," she could barely whisper, "pregnant..."

"He beat you like this because you're pregnant?"

Agnes nodded her head, too exhausted to speak anymore.

"I'm getting you help," Jack's voice trembled. Agnes couldn't muster the strength to contest, even if she had wanted to.

He returned through the attic access, gently replacing the cover as he left, and slipped back into his own cottage. Jack thought about going to the local police, but he knew it would be futile. Most of the police in the small village were drinking buddies with Blake, and the effort would get him nowhere, except to be fired. Instead, he decided to try and get help from Agnes's parents. Jack sprinted the familiar path between his cottage, and the small house where Agnes had been recovering just a few months ago. He ran the coastal path into the town, his chest burning by the time he'd arrived. Doubled over and struggling to catch his breath, he knocked feverishly on the door. Her father answered.

"Jack," he said surprised, "what brings you here?"

"It's Agnes," Jack stammered, breathless, "Blake's beat her. Badly this time."

"Oh my," his eyes became heavy with sadness, "what can I do?"

"You need to get her away from him," Jack demanded, "bring her home. Help her leave. Something."

"I can't," her father said wearily.

"What do you mean you can't? Why not?"

"I've known Blake for a long time. It's best I don't interfere."

"We're talking about your daughter here, sir."

"Don't you think I know that" her father snapped, "If I could help, then I would. Blake paid off a tremendous debt for me, years ago, with the agreement that he could Mary my daughter. If I do anything to break up that marriage, I'll be as good as dead. Now run along," he motioned away from his house.

"Unbelievable," Jack scoffed, "your daughter is laying beaten by her husband, with an unborn child, and you're not going to so much as lift a finger because you're scared?"

Agnes' father stood silent, caught off guard by the news of his daughter's pregnancy and the idea of a grandchild on the way. "I knew his father, and I know him," he finally spoke, "they're violent people Jack. The best thing you can do is not get in their way. I'm sure he'll calm down and apologise. Agnes will be fine, she's a strong woman."

"He will kill her John"

"It's better if she just stays. Trust me," her father said, beginning to close the door, "I'm sorry I couldn't be more helpful."

Just as Jack lunged towards the door, the door clicked shut and the metallic sounds of locks jingling could be heard.

Jack made the hike back to the lighthouse with the cowardice of Agnes' father fresh in his mind, making each step into an assault on the ground beneath him. When he got back to the cottage, he knocked on Agnes's door, and this time she answered.

He snuck in quickly and found Ben was there.

"Don't panic," Ben said slowly, "Blake is unconscious".

"Sit down Jack. We have a plan to protect Agnes for at least the next week." Ben continued "Agnes is going to go into town and pretend she is seeing someone to deal with her 'situation', just like Blake told her to. This will give us some time. She can stay with her parents for the week."

. . .

"No," Jack exclaimed, "they want nothing to do with it. I'm sorry Agnes, but I've just spoken with them."

AGNES PUT her head in her hands and cried. Her life really was not worth living. Wherever she went, he would find her. She knew it.

BACK IN HIS LITTLE COTTAGE, Jack thumbed through the diary that Agnes had entrusted him with. He read page after page of abuse from Blake. Jack wraps the diary back up, imagining what Blake would do if he realised that Agnes kept it, or worse, that he himself now had it. In his bedroom, he pulled up a floorboard, one that he had known to be loose, and tucked the little black journal neatly underneath it, making a note in his mind to remind Agnes that he still had it. Jack waited, plagued by worry for Agnes, and loathing for Blake, until a time in the evening when he knew that Blake would have returned home, and Ben would be manning the tower, before ascending the staircase, and joining in Ben's watch.

. . .

"What are we going to do?" Ben asked, "We could go to the police?"

Jack shook his head. "I think that's a bad idea. Most of them spend their time drinking with Blake. They love him, they wouldn't do a thing."

"I will kill that man, Jack; I promise you that."

"Ben, we both know you can't do that. He's a larger man and you'd ruin your own life anyways."

"I think," Jack began to whisper, "that we need to find a way to get her out of here, away from him. She needs to disappear."

"Alright," Ben resigned, "but how in the bloody hell do we do that? And without Blake knowing that we had anything to do with it?"

"That's the tricky part," Jack admitted, "we need to think of something though, and quick."

The two men spent the entire night in the tower together, trying to formulate any plot to try and get Agnes away, without Blake knowing that they were involved at all. In the matter of a few hours, they formulated a plan. They would wait, Jack figured, until a night when Blake had gone to town and was sure to get liquored up heavily. Jack planned on having his fiancé, Sarah, arrange for a car to come to the cliffs and pick up Agnes, who could stay with her for a little while, until they could find a more permanent solution- somewhere completely off the island, they figured. They would need her to write a note, something simple about how she couldn't take the abuse anymore and had simply left, with no indication of where she had gone. The hardest part, they figured, would be to get Agnes to agree to getting out of here.

"I'll talk to her," Ben stated, when they had finished imagining their plan, "I can convince her to leave, that she'll be safe."

"Alright," Jack agreed, "tomorrow, when Blake's back on, I'll make sure he doesn't come down. I'll stay up here in the morning for a bit, keep him distracted."

The next morning, they set the first part of their plot into motion. Ben woke early, listening for the sound of Blake leaving his cottage for the day. A few moments later, he went straight to his attic, and across to Agnes. He found her, asleep when he approached the bed.

"Agnes," he whispered, "how are you feeling."

"If it didn't hurt so much, I would be smiling," she whispered, "I'm so glad to see you."

"Listen," he placed his hands over hers, "Jack told me about the baby. We're going to get you out of here, both of you."

"There's nowhere to go."

"I have a plan," Ben whispered, "I'll get it all set up, a place for you to stay for a while, a way to get you away from that monster for good, I promise."

Agnes shook her head in disagreement.

"Please don't fight me on this, Agnes," Ben pleaded, "do it for the baby. You know if you stay, you'll likely both wind up dead. I can't even bear to think it."

Agnes began to weep as she thought about the implications of remaining in the house, she remembered Blakes words, *get rid of it, or I will*. She knew Ben and Jack were right. If she didn't leave, she couldn't protect her baby from the grips of such a monster.

"Alright," Agnes nodded, "how will we do it?"

"Listen," Ben started, "no matter what happens, you can't tell anyone anything. Not a living soul, ok?"

"Ok," Agnes agreed.

Ben kept his voice at a whisper, as he divulged the grand plan to Agnes, down to the smallest of details. He had dates and times, locations and pathways, everything mapped out in his mind. Agnes followed along, listening intently and trying to carefully log every part in her mind, anxious that she would forget a pivotal step. Nervous as she was, when Ben had finished explaining how things would unfold, she couldn't help but be excited at the possibility of freedom, of not living in fear, of not being assaulted. She relished it. By the end of the conversation, Agnes was fully committed to placing her fate in Ben's hands with unwavering faith. All that she had to do was to wait for the right time, and she was certain she would have the world.

"Listen," Ben whispered, "I'll get notes to you, ok? On days when Blake's on duty, listen for a knock from the attic. If you hear a knock, there will be a note for you. I'll drop it through, but you need to promise me that you'll hide them, somewhere he'll never look."

"Why can't we just talk?" Agnes challenged.

"We can't risk anyone overhearing anything. When I know it's safe, we'll talk, but you need to do whatever I ask you to in those letters, ok?"

Agnes nodded her head in agreement.

"And remember, hide them, always hide them."

"I will," Agnes promised. As Ben stood to leave, she called to him.

"Ben?"

"Yeah?"

"Thank you," she smiled, "for everything."

Ben smiled back at her and disappeared.

In the days that followed, Ben did exactly as he had promised. Though he never did find an opportunity with which he felt safe to slip into her cottage and see her, he would write long notes to Agnes, outlining certain aspects of how he intended to get her away from this cliffside hell. When Blake would take his watch, Ben would pull himself quietly into the attic, and softly knock after he had slipped the envelope through the small wooden access door. He would keep his ear pressed against this cover, listening to be sure that Agnes had retrieved the note, each time leaving a warm feeling that washed over his heart, knowing that she was one step closer to being free, to being happy.

A week went by like this, a clandestine orchestration of a great escape, communicated through hidden message. Everything appeared so easy on the surface. It would be flawless, so long as Agnes placed her faith in the words written. At the end of that week, a warm front had rolled into the area, providing a break from the cool, brisk Autumn temperatures, bringing with it a thick, early morning fog. Ben was on duty, closely studying any movement in the sea, knowing how treacherous the shore waters could get with such low visibility. Standing on the balcony, the sight of movement on the ground drew his attention to the edge of the property, where a sheer cliff met with the beating waves, sixty or seventy feet down. It was Agnes, surely out to enjoy the warming air, and take in the sea. Ben smiled, watching her as she rubbed her stomach. A shimmer in the sea distracted him for a mere fraction of a second, and when his vision returned, Agnes was gone. He was startled by the quickness with which she had vanished, as the distance between the edge of the property and the tower was just grass and rocks and there were no structures for Agnes to be hidden by, and she couldn't have possibly moved quickly enough to get back to the cottages. He began calling her name, shouting "Agnes" from the top of the tower, loudly enough that it drew Jack's attention.

"What's wrong?" Jacked called up from the base of the lighthouse.

"Agnes," Ben called back, pointing to the edge of the drop, "I swear I just saw her standing there, and then suddenly she wasn't."

"What do you mean she wasn't?"

"I was distracted for a fraction of a second," Ben yelled, "when I looked back, she was just gone."

"Maybe she went home?" Jack asked.

"I don't think so," Ben stated, "she can't move that fast. I would have seen."

"I'll check," Jack said.

Jack knocked on the door of Agnes's cabin, which was answered by Blake.

"What do you want," Blake growled.

"Is Agnes home?" Jack asked.

"Why do you care where she is?"

"Well," Jack rolled his eyes, "it's just that Ben just saw her over by the cliffs. He said she was there, and then suddenly she was just gone."

Blake shut the door in Jack's face, and returned a few moments late, "well, she isn't here."

"Thanks."

Blake shut the door. Jack spent half an hour searching around the grounds for Agnes, but with no success. After searching, he sprinted to the top of the tower.

"Are you sure you saw Agnes?" Jack asked.

"I'm bloody positive," Ben answered in a panic, "she was standing right there. I turned around and she was just gone. I mean fractions of a second gone, Jack. Did you check if she's home?"

"She's not," Jack shook his head, "I checked everywhere else too. I didn't find her."

"Shit," Ben said, becoming even more anxious, "let's check again."

The two men spent the afternoon hunting for Agnes but had no luck in finding her. They scoured the property in its entirety; Jack even slipped into the attic, just in case she had hidden herself up there. Ben pedalled his bicycle as hard as he could into town, when he returned, he explained to Jack he had searched through all of it: her parents' house, every little local store and every park. Blake scarcely showed his face; and instead remained at his post in the light tower, the room thick with tobacco smoke and the smell of whiskey. The next day, Jack notified the police. The police took reports from all three men and conducted their own inspections and found nothing. Jack kept a suspicious glare glued to Blake all day, who only smirked and smiled back. Jack was sure that Blake had, just as he said he would, killed Agnes.

CHAPTER
SEVEN

"It was so great to meet you," Daisy said gleefully, "and thank you for cooking such a lovely meal."

"Anytime," Danny replied with a beaming smile, "it was fantastic to finally get to meet the lady Emily's talked so much about."

The two exchanged handshakes, and Danny headed for the door, Emily followed him.

"See ya, Danny," Shelly called, and gave a little wave.

"Bye Shelly" Danny gave a little nod and disappeared outside with Emily. A few moments later, Emily reentered.

"I guess it's just us ladies now."

"Yeah," Daisy said, uneasily darting her eyes

around the room. In the absence of Danny, and the sunlight, and the distraction of conversation, the uneasiness from the events of the night before settled back in, weighing heavily on her. Emily picked up on this immediately.

"What's the matter Daisy?", she inquired.

"Aren't you at all uncomfortable in here, after everything that happened last night and this morning mum?"

"I'm sure it's nothing," Emily offered, "the more I think about it, it's probably just our imagination playing tricks on us."

"Mum," Daisy challenged, removing the old photograph from her pocket, "you said you've seen this woman in your dreams! There's no way you've ever seen her before, the photograph is years old."

"Maybe I saw a photograph of her sometime and I've just forgotten," Emily tried to sound reassuring.

"I don't know Emily," Shelly chimed in, "it's a bit freaky that you've been seeing this woman in your dreams, especially when you consider everything else that's been going on."

"Nobody ever even found out what happened to her," Daisy interjected.

"What do you mean?"

"Shelly and I found this old article," Daisy

removed the folded-up copy, and slid it in front of Emily, "this woman, Agnes, just disappeared in nineteen twenty-four, without a trace. And then look, her husband, Blake, the man I saw last night, killed himself."

"Right after his best friend died in a freak accident," Shelly added.

"So, what," Emily asked, reluctantly with a chuckle, "you think their spirits are in the cottage now?"

"I don't know," Daisy answered, "but I know what I saw last night, and I know that I'm uneasy here."

"And" Shelly interrupted, "you know there's been some weird stuff happening here. Now you're seeing a woman, in your dreams, who went missing from this very cottage a hundred years ago? You must admit, it's at least strange."

Emily sighed, "Yes, I'll agree that it's a bit strange, but what's the sense in worrying about it?"

"Actually," Daisy cleared her throat, "Shelly has an idea."

Emily and Daisy both shifted their eyes to Shelly, who took a long drink of wine before speaking. "You would both have to be very open-minded," she insisted. "My mum, she runs a spiritualist church.

It's a place for people who are spiritually sensitive, so-to-speak. They have all these insightful mediums there."

"Mediums?" Emily asked, "like psychics?"

"Not quite," Shelly laughed, "they don't read minds, or see into the future, or anything like that. They're just very intuitive when it comes to the living, and they have a special kind of connection to the afterlife. Just come once. I'll introduce you to Debbie, she's one of the best. You can tell her about everything that's been happening, and about the dreams, and maybe she can help."

"I don't know," Emily's voice was skeptical.

"I know," Shelly said assuredly, "it sounds crazy, but listen, spirits really do get trapped. It happens all the time, especially in older places like yours. It would be worth talking to them, and at least letting them come by."

"Please, mum," Daisy begged.

"The worst thing that could happen," Shelly added, "is that you waste an afternoon. What's the harm?"

"I suppose," Emily conceded, after several moments of silent thinking.

"It's tomorrow evening, I can pick you up if you'd like?" Shelly said with a buzz of excitement.

The three all agreed on the plan, and the night passed without incident. Daisy slept in her mum's bedroom, like a young child during a heavy storm, blanketed in the dull sound of late-night television. They rose early, and spent the day in the café, impatient for the time when they could close the shop and make their visit to Shelly's mother's church. The afternoon came, and the sign that hung on the glass front door was turned around. The three women piled into Shelly's car, and she began to weave the windy roads of the old village. After nearly thirty minutes of driving, they had arrived.

Hidden away at the end of a small, worn gravel road sat a Victorian brick building, the structure stood alone, imposing and beautiful, against a backdrop of seemingly endless greenery. 'Four Mile Bridge Village Hall' supported an antiquated huge brass door knocker on a big wooden door. Shelly parked her car in a large, graveled square, next to the only other vehicle in sight, and excitedly led Emily and Daisy towards the hall, following the pathway created by the large, flat stones, slightly mossed over and sinking from the decades of use. The wooden doors opened with a loud creaking, which echoed through hall.

"I'm sorry," a woman's voice called out, unseen, "the service doesn't start for another hour."

"I know, mum," Shelly called back out.

"Shelly?" The voice shouted joyfully, as a woman came into view from the far corner.

"Hey mum," She smiled gleefully, spreading her arms for a hug. The resemblance was uncanny. Emily knew immediately that this must have been Shelly's mother, with the same curvy figure and brilliant smile. The woman's long hair was nested in a messy bun, her eyes as big and as green as Shelly's.

"You must be Ruth," Emily said.

"I am," Ruth replied with a big smile, "you must be psychic? You'll definitely fit in around here."

The four women all laughed in unison. "Oh no," Emily said, still chuckling, "I've heard a lot about you, and you two bear a remarkable resemblance."

"And I suppose you're Emily?" She responded with a nod. "I wish I looked half as beautiful as my little girl. How's the Coffee shop? I hope Shelly isn't drinking through your stock!"

"Oh stop, mum," Shelly blushed, "this is Emily's daughter, Daisy. Daisy's visiting from London."

"It's a pleasure to meet you both," Ruth said, holding a smile, "welcome to our hall" she said, with an overexaggerated arm gesture.

"Thank you," Emily and Daisy said in synchronization.

"So, Shelly has been telling me you have been having some strange happenings at your little cottage."

"Well yes I suppose we have, but I doubt it's all caused by a ghost" Emily said.

"No," Ruth laughed, "I would say not one, but two ghosts"

Emily was a little taken a back and wasn't sure if Ruth was picking up on something already or if Shelly had told her about Blake and Agnus.

"I'll ask Debbie to stop back after the service and have a chat with you, she is much better than I am" Ruth smiled but she seemed to be looking through Emily.

"What exactly is that they do?" Daisy asked with curiosity, "I mean, I've heard of mediums in books, and movies, and all of that. But I've never really known any in real life."

"Well, Daisy," Ruth started, "as spiritualists, we believe that an individual's awareness- that is, their consciousness- continues after death. Since this consciousness doesn't die with the body, they still maintain the ability to communicate. That's what mediums excel at. Mediums have an extremely heightened sensitivity to the spiritual and a special connection to different planes of existence. This allows them, with a lot of work, to be able to communicate with the consciousness that remains living, even after death in the physical world."

"That sounds amazing," Daisy said in awe.

"It really does," Emily agreed.

"It's ok to be skeptical," Ruth said with a smile, placing her warm hands-on Emily's.

"Mediums," Shelly said with a laugh, "also have very strong intuition about the living."

"It's just new to me, is all," Emily blushed.

"You should watch the service," Ruth insisted, "I'll introduce you to Debbie afterward."

"That sounds wonderful, thank you," Daisy chimed.

By this time, people had begun to pour into the church, taking their seats which lined either side of the church, in perfectly aligned rows. Emily, Daisy, and Shelly all took seats near the front, while Ruth disappeared into a room at the back of the building. The building filled with the deep hum of conversations amongst the congregation, at least forty strong already, more than Emily or Daisy would have guessed, all patiently waiting for Ruth to take the podium, and deliver the evening's message. Emily sat near the end of the pew, with Daisy in between her and Shelly. A woman took a seat on the pew, next to Emily. She was older, short and petite. Her long grey hair was left down, rolling over her shoulders and flowing halfway down her back. Emily could feel the fixation of her eyes, light blue and dulled by time. Even when Emily would turn her head to look at her, she kept her gaze rigid. Minutes passed like this, developing a discomfort in Emily.

"I'm sorry," she said, finally blinking away her stare, "you have a lot going on hun."

"Beg your pardon," Emily asked, politely and confused.

"It can be tricky business," the woman said, her voice raspy, "dealing with the dead. There's a lot of uneasiness that comes with all the strange goings on. You've had a lot of curious things happening at your house, haven't you?"

"How could you possibly know that?" Emily whispered harshly, "did Shelly put you up to this?"

"No, no dear," the woman insisted, "I don't mean to upset you. It's hard to explain, but when a person is encountering spirits, the energy becomes sort of attached to them. And so, the conduit moves with the individual, and I can see some of the things, even without being in the place myself."

"I think the service is about to start," Emily whispered, trying to change the subject.

"Blake," the woman muttered, "he was killed you know? He's not happy at all that you're living in his house."

Emily was speechless.

"How do you know that name?" Daisy half whispered, half shouted, overhearing the conversation.

"Hi Debbie," Shelly suddenly exclaimed, recognizing the woman sitting next to Emily.

"Did you hear what she just said?" Daisy asked excitedly.

"I couldn't hear over the crowd," Shelly laughed.

"She said she knows there's strange things happening at my mum's cottage, and that a man named Blake was killed, and doesn't like my mum being in his cottage!"

"I told you she was good," Shelly exclaimed.

"Which one of you," the woman, Debbie, started again, "has this Blake been touching on the shoulder," she paused, closing her eyes, "at the top of the stairs?"

"Not me," Daisy stated, Emily remained silent, and simply shook her head no.

"Well," Debbie rasped "be careful. The spirit of this man is dark, and powerful enough to manifest in more physical means. Things like certain unexpected scents and noises. You may even see him as an apparition. He's looking for someone, someone who was taken from him. It's the reason why he can't cross over."

"Agnes!" Daisy spat out.

Even as a skeptic, the words of this woman made Emily very discomforted.

"The service is about to start," the woman whispered, "after maybe we can chat if you'd like."

"Yes," Emily said, "that would be great. We came to see you."

"Wonderful," the woman smiled, and Ruth approached the podium.

Ruth captivated the crowd during the service, discussing her thoughts on the afterlife, and the various planes of existence, and went into depth about how trauma could anchor the consciousness of those who expired to the physical world. She then invited a medium called Jessica to come and take the podium to demonstrate some mediumship. She gave some incredible messages to several people. Emily and Daisy shared how much they learned, and the impressiveness of Jessica's messages. When she concluded her messages Ruth bid the congregation a good night, and made a waving motion at Shelly, which she understood as the request to bring Emily, Daisy, and Debbie into the little office room she had, situated in the very far corner of the building. A request to which she obliged with a smile.

"I see you've met Debbie," Ruth said, slightly breathless from her performance.

"We have," Emily replied with a nod.

"She already knew about what we came here to talk about," Daisy added, surprise in her voice, "I can't believe it."

"Well," Ruth chimed, "that's probably more common than you think, especially with mediums as good as Debbie."

"So, you guys are psychics?" Shelly chuckled.

"Oh no, no," Ruth laughed, "it's more of an intuition thing, like certain feelings that we get, which help us have better foresight, so-to-speak."

"Ruth," Debbie interrupted, "there is a spirit stuck in the little cottage that Emily now lives in. He's very dark. I can sense it, just by the energy around this woman, without even being in the home. This Blake, he is very, very angry.

He's stuck in this physical world, bound by someone who has gone missing. Agnes, I think is what this pretty young lady said her name might be."

"Do you think it's malevolent," Ruth asked, her voice serious and slow.

"It could be," Debbie nodded, "there's a lot of anger in this woman's house."

"Like dangerous?" Daisy asked anxiously.

"Not necessarily," Debbie answered, "but it is possible."

"I'm new to all of this," Emily inserted, realizing how aggravated her voice was, she added, "I'm sorry. This is just a lot to take in."

"It's ok," Ruth said, "don't be sorry. I know this is new for you, and not something that you're completely convinced about. It's very unsettling, I know."

"Thank you," Emily replied, a small tear forming in the corner of her eye.

"Can you help?" Daisy asked, her question directed at Debbie.

"I can try," Debbie said.

"How does it work?" Daisy asked, "what do you do, I mean."

"Well," Ruth took to answering, "we will do

some research, check our own archives, and try and find out who, exactly, we're dealing with."

"Oh," Daisy interrupted, fishing the folded article out of her pocket, "take this, maybe it will help you. It's about Blake and Agnes, and some others who used to live and work at the lighthouse."

"Thank you," Ruth said, eyeing over the article, "this is a great start. I'll see if we can find anything else. It's best to know who the spirit was, and exactly why they're still here. It can help us communicate with them better and, more importantly, try and help guide their consciousness to the next plane of existence, which is much easier if you know exactly why they're stuck. Once we've found as much possible information as we can, we'll come to your house, and do a number of things, starting with trying to communicate with the spirit and cleanse the quarters. Only, of course, if you're alright with it Emily."

"Mum," Daisy whispered, "you should let them. It can't hurt."

Emily pondered for a moment, the eyes of all the women on her, waiting. "You know what," she finally answered, "let's give it a shot."

"Lovely," Ruth said, "how about the Monday

after next? Two weeks should give us plenty of time. Does that work for you?"

"That should be perfect," Emily smiled.

"Mum," Shelly spoke, "I'd be glad to help with the background information. Daisy and I already did some digging," she motioned towards the article that her mother held.

"I can help too," Daisy quickly added.

"That would be fantastic," Ruth said, "it's local, so we might even have some information in the church's archives. They've been keeping documents there for centuries."

The conversation ended, and Shelly delivered Emily and Daisy back home. Over the next several days, things remained relatively normal. Emily would spend her day in the coffee shop, and allowed Shelly to take Daisy to the church, nearly every day, to dig through old newspapers, property deeds, personal letters, and the myriads of other local historical documents that the parish had accumulated over the years. Things remained relatively quiet in the small little cottage, enough so that even Daisy had become comfortable. Small things would happen, a flickering light, or a creaking board in the attic, but they were things that Emily could easily explain away as simply being traits of the old house, still not wanting to completely embrace the idea that her little cottage could be haunted. Danny even began showing up in the afternoons, continuing to try and make small repairs and often joining them both for dinner and a few drinks.

Even then, Daisy was counting the days until Debbie and Ruth would come and cleanse the house, mostly for the sake of her mum. While her time was limited, and soon she would be parting with the company of her mother to resume her studies in London, she wanted to be sure that her mum would be safe after she had left. A week had passed since their visit to Ruth's church, and the two were up late, drinking and talking into the night, both honouring the silent agreement they had developed to keep the conversation light while in the cottage. Chatting about school, Daisy's future plans, and her imminent return to London, their conversation abruptly stopped; both women becoming dead silent, as they heard the familiar sound of the steel dead-bolt lock of the front becoming unlocked. They watched in terror as the lock rotated and slid back.

"What the," Daisy gasped.

Emily watched in awe as the deadbolt became unlocked, and the brass knob of the front door slowly began to rotate, with a slow, high-pitched, agonising squeal. Emily was speechless as the door became unlatched, and slowly opened into the cottage, letting an icy breeze fill the room. The door opened at a slow pace, the creaking of the old wood filling the entire cottage. The panic set in, like being buried alive by fear.

"Who's there," Emily called out loudly, aggressively, forcing herself to be brave.

The door stopped momentarily, a shudder rolling across Emily's entire body.

"I said," Emily yelled this time, "who's there?"

"Mum, don't," Daisy insisted, panicked.

A few seconds later, the door resumed its slow swing. It was everything Emily could do to muster the courage to stand, looking behind the door to see if there was someone opening it from the outside. Seeing only moonlight, she swallowed the lump that had formed in her throat, and slowly approached the door. The room filled with the smell of burning tobacco.

"Mum," Daisy whispered in a shaky voice, "maybe we should just go."

"There's nowhere to go," Emily snapped, "it's too late, anyway."

Reaching the door, Emily peered outside, once

again seeing nothing and nobody. She slowly reached out to grab the brass knob when the door, suddenly and violently, slammed shut. Emily jumped back in a gasp, the sudden noise causing a high-pitched wail to escape her throat. She threw herself onto the door, forcing the deadbolt lock back into position before rushing back to the sofa where Daisy sat, and wrapping her arms around her tightly. The house fell silent, save for the heavy breathing of Daisy, muffled by her mum's chest. Tears formed in Emily's eyes as she began to hear the stairs creaking, one at a time, as if some tremendous weight ascended them, slowly, one by one. She tried to keep Daisy's ears covered, and listened as the noise moved up the stairs, and down the hallway. The noise came to a stop directly above their heads; the room where Daisy had been staying. She kept Daisy's head pulled in tight, her ears covered, until the noise didn't return for several minutes.

"It's alright, Daisy," she whispered, "we're fine."

"Mum," she cried, "we can't stay here tonight."

"I don't have anywhere to take you," Emily said, her voice apologetic, "it's two in the morning. We'll be fine, I promise. Tomorrow, we'll try and make arrangements."

Daisy understood and nodded her head in agreement. Emily tried to keep her own terror as well hidden as she could as she walked to the small storage cupboard, built under the steps, for the blankets. In passing by the stairs, her attention was caught by the pools of water that had formed on every step, as if someone had walked through the house with wet boots. She passed the stairs rapidly, making haste to get the blankets, and returned to the couch with Daisy. To keep Daisy calm, she didn't mention the strange and sudden appearance of the water spots, and instead turned the television on, and kept the volume up loud, as they held each other. The noise stopped, the smell of tobacco faded away, just as suddenly as it had appeared. The two remained close on the sofa and fought to drift off to sleep. Daisy was woken from her sleep by the sound of her mother gasping.

"Mum," she said sleepily, "mum, are you alright?"

"I'm fine," Emily said, trying to catch her breath, "just a nightmare."

"What about?"

"Nothing," Emily tried to insist.

"What was it mum?" Daisy continued to prod.

"I saw that woman again," Emily resigned, knowing she wouldn't ever drop it, "she was on the floor, curling herself up, her arms wrapped around her stomach. I could hear a man's voice shouting at her, but it was muffled. It was like I was seeing everything from someone else's eyes. Like I was actually there, like I told you before."

"God, mum," Daisy said, "I can't wait until Debbie and Ruth come here."

"Honestly," Emily tried to smile, "neither can I."

The two managed to drift back off to sleep, and stayed this way soundly, sleeping several hours into the morning. Daisy woke first, noticing the labored breathing and quiet moans of her sleeping mother. She contemplated waking her up, but before she could make the decision, Emily shot awake. This time it was different. Emily didn't wake up in a gasp. Instead, she woke up in a shrill scream, almost as if in pain, like one would scream if they were branded by a hot iron.

"What?" Daisy yelled, startled, "what is it? What is it?"

"Another bloody nightmare," Emily conceded.

"What was it this time?"

"It was different this time, Daisy. You don't want to hear it."

"I do, mum."

"Maybe tomorrow," Emily insisted, kissing her daughter on the forehead, "get a little more sleep."

Daisy rolled her eyes. Emily laid down, but each time she closed them she would relive this nightmare. She was in the observation room, at the very top of the lighthouse. There was a heavy storm, she could see the lighting crack over the sea. As in her other ones, it was as if she was there herself, this time standing on the balcony. On the balcony, in her dream, Emily was watching a man, young and tall. She saw his face; the man had a ruggedly handsome look about him. Suddenly, just as the man turned to face her, the man goes over the handrail of the balcony of the lighthouse. Worse yet, it's as if Daisy pushed the man over herself. She remembers dreaming, walking over to the handrail and leaning over the small railing. Looking down, she could see the body of this man, lifeless and stiff. Even in the darkness of the nightmare, in the bright flashes of lightning, she was certain she could see the blood running from the man's body, whoever he was.

CHAPTER
EIGHT

Bags formed under Emily's eyes in the days leading up to when Debbie and Ruth would visit the cottage.

SHE HAD COMPLETELY SUBMITTED to the idea that the old cottage was indefinitely plagued by something; something all the logic in the world couldn't reconcile. At night, her and Daisy would be startled awake by the sudden, inexplicable sound of the old wooden steps creaking, or the residual noise from the slam of a door somewhere in the cottage. No matter how frequently things would happen, neither of them could get used to it. Worse yet, for Emily, even in her sleep she was uneasy.

. . .

Nearly every night, she would sleep as if she were awake in someone else's body. Sometimes it was as if she herself were a participant in the moment, other times she was a wallflower, merely watching things unfold. Even the perceivably good moments, like when her slumbering brain conjured the image of the same woman it frequently did, was in the throes of love, at the height of ecstasy, she would still wake feeling uneasy, dizzy and nauseous. It wasn't just the woman from the photograph anymore though. Emily had begun seeing fragments of the man, Blake, and two other men. One with long, sandy blonde hair, tall with icy blue eyes, and another man still, young and thin with near black hair.

Sometimes she would dream of the woman crying, terrified of something, as she had done before. Other times she would see the husband, feet propped on the same little wooden table that still sat in the room at the top of the tower, with a bitter look on his bearded face, smoking from that familiar pipe. None were worse, though, than the ones in which she saw the falling man, plummeting to a demise all that distance down from the top of the lighthouse.

Even in her waking hours, the sound of his body hitting rang in her ears incessantly, and she could never shake the feeling of guilt, certain that she had pushed him over the railing herself. It was the very dream she had refused to tell Daisy.

The melancholy of it all was intensely magnified the day Daisy brought home the old newspaper. Daisy had been spending her days with Shelly, splitting their time between the basement of the church, digging through monumental amounts of records and newspapers, and Shelly's apartment, scouring the internet for anything they could find on the inhabitants that had lived there over the years. In the days of research, they had agreed to stay focused on Blake and his crew.

In the decades that the lighthouse had been in operation, it seemed that the span of years during which Blake had been the head keeper was the only time when any tragedy had occurred. As Debbie and Ruth ensured, these types of supernatural occurrences could almost always be traced back to events that were indicative of trauma. Beyond this, Daisy retained that her mother was certain she had been seeing Agnes in her dreams.

EMILY HAD JUST ARRIVED home from the shop and was sitting at her small dining table waiting for Danny to arrive and nursing a glass of wine when Daisy arrived home.

"Mum," she said, "we finally found some more information about the men that lived here, back in the 20's, when Agnes went missing."

"Really?" Emily asked curiously.

"Well," Daisy responded apprehensively, "I'm not sure if I'd call it new information per say. We already knew all these people lived and worked here, Blake and Agnes Conaway, Benjamin Campbell, and Jack Lawson, but this article is an interesting write up about what happened back then. How Agnes went missing, and Jack's accident, Blake's suicide, all of it. And check this out," Daisy placed a photocopy of an old newspaper on the table in front of Emily, "it has pictures of all of them too."

Emily gasped.

"What is it, mum?"

"It's nothing," Emily stuttered, grappling to hold her composure.

"It's not nothing, I can tell."

"It's just," Emily relented, tears falling against the photocopy.

"It's just what?" Daisy persisted.

"This man," Emily placed her finger on the photo of a man, "who is he?"

"That's Jack," Daisy said with a confused tone, "why?"

"What happened to him?"

"He had an accident," Daisy answered, "he fell from the balcony of the lighthouse."

Emily's tears began to blur the ink on the page.

"Why," Daisy persisted, pulling the page from the path of her mum's tears.

"Do you remember the other night, when I woke up screaming? The nightmare I wouldn't tell you about?"

"How could I forget?"

"It's one that I keep having. In it, I see this man," Emily choked up, swallowed, and forced herself on, "I've seen him fall from the top of the tower."

Daisy sat stunned.

"It's going to sound ridiculous," Emily paused, "but in the dream, even after I wake up, I can't shake this feeling that he was pushed over the handrail."

Just then, both women jump, startled by a loud knocking on the front door.

"I'm coming," Emily calls out, drying her eyes. Daisy struggles to catch her breath from the fright. Moments later, Emily returns with Danny.

"Hi Danny," Daisy manages, "tea?"

"Hey there," Danny smiles, "yes please Dais. Are you two alright? Seems pretty heavy in here."

"We're fine," Emily tried to sound assuring, "we're just reading about the people who worked this lighthouse, back in the twenties."

"Interesting," Danny says, picking up the photocopied newspaper, his eyes quickly shifting along the rows of words, "I was just talking to my mum and dad about all of this. This man here, Ben, he's my great grandad."

"Did you ever know him?" Daisy quickly asked.

"Regretfully not," Danny shook his head, "my dad of course did though. Sounds like he was a wonderful man. Funny though, my dad said Ben talked a lot about these fellows that he worked with. He said that his grandfather would always say that things weren't what people thought, and he always wished he could tell him what had really happened."

"Are you serious?" Daisy asked, astonished.

"I am. Why are you so interested in this anyway?" Danny asked

"I've been having some really strange nightmares," Emily admitted, reluctantly, "and in them, I see these men, and this woman, Agnes."

"Well," Danny said, his voice pragmatic, "it's not uncommon to have nightmares, especially when there's a lot of stress and big changes in your life."

"Except I've only seen Agnes and Blake in an old photo that fell out of this book and now Ben and Jack when Daisy brought this old newspaper home., but I have seen them in my dreams"

"Are you sure?" Danny asked, "Maybe you've caught glimpses somewhere when you did research on this place?"

"No," Emily blurted, "I really didn't."

"And what about all of the weird stuff that happens here?" Daisy interjected.

"It's an old building," Danny said, "but I have to admit there are a lot of odd things happening here that I can't explain, and I have heard many a ghost story told about this old place."

Emily was taken aback, "What stories Danny, why haven't you said anything before?"

"I didn't want to scare you; you'd just moved here. I also didn't want you to think I was trying to get close to you by making you feel you couldn't be alone here." Danny sipped the tea that Daisy passed to him.

"We're having the house cleansed in a few days. With the move, I can't afford a room anywhere else right now. Would you stay with us, just until then? I would feel a lot better if you did. What do you think Daisy?"

Daisy nodded in agreement.

"A Clearing, really?" Danny looked worried, "Well, I don't know about all of that, but I'd be happy to stay if it'll make you feel better."

"Thank you, Danny," Emily forced a small smile.

The three had dinner and a few glasses of wine that night. Danny kept the conversation steered away from the history of the lighthouse, trying to keep the women from thinking too much about Emily's nightmares, or the strange things they would hear through the night. The evening slunk by without so much as a board creaking. Emily and Daisy were glad for the distraction, and content that Danny's presence really did seem to dull the strange things out at the cottage. Daisy was the first to take advantage of the unassuming nature of the evening and welcome an uninterrupted night's sleep. Danny and Emily continued their conversation a while longer, until Emily's eyes burned with tiredness.

"I'm sorry," Emily finally conceded with a long yawn, "I think I have to get some sleep."

"Of course," Danny said, bearing his same wide smile, "I'll take the couch."

"Actually," Emily blushed, "would you mind sleeping upstairs with me? Only if it's not too strange."

"Absolutely fine by me," Danny winked, "I'd be happy to."

Emily fell asleep quickly in the comfort of the warmth of Danny's body heat and the steady, rhythmic sound of his breath against her ear. With her head heavy on his chest, Danny slipped into a slumber shortly after.

Danny's eyes opened wide with confusion, not quite comprehending why he had just woken. He gently repositioned Emily, who remained quiet and asleep. Danny rolled on his side, fumbling in the darkness for his watch, which was laid on the small table next to the bed. Squinting, he could make out the positions of the dark hands in the glow; two twenty-two in the morning. Just as he rolled onto his back, closing his eyes, they were jolted open by the distinct sound of a knocking on the front the door. He waited a few moments, certain that his ears were playing tricks on him, before the knocking noise echoed through the still house once again. Careful not to wake Emily, Danny slid quietly out of the bed, the knocking noise coming again before he had his jeans on. At the top of the stairs, Danny stopped, glancing through the half-open door of Daisy's room; he could see that Daisy was still sound asleep. Just as he was about to descend the stairs, his body became completely still. He could feel an icy grip on his shoulders, sending chills through him that caused all his hair to stand on end. He began to turn his head, expecting to see Emily standing behind him. Before he could, he felt a force push against his shoulders so hard that there was no way he could stop himself. He fell violently down the stairs, each step like a punch to his body. When he finally came to a stop at the bottom, shooting his eyes to the top of the stairs; there was no one. He waited, certain that the sound of his body tumbling to the bottom would have woken one, if not both, of the sleeping women, but neither appeared. He was distracted by the sudden return of the sound of knocking on the front door, immediately behind him. With a rush of adrenaline, he quickly turned and flung the door open whilst turning on the exterior light in one, simultaneous movement. The cold night air washed over his bare torso as he stepped outside, quickly surveying every direction in search of whoever had been knocking, but the night was still. There was no glimpse of a shadow, no sound of shuffling footsteps from a running perpetrator. Only the ever so slight breeze, and the familiar quietness of the early morning hours. He hobbled back into the hall to see both Emily and Daisy appear at the top of the stairs, talking over one another.

"What the hell happened Danny, are you ok?" Emily was shouting as she ran down the stairs to be next to him. He gathered himself as quickly as he could. "I am ok, just bruised I think. But get your stuff, you're coming to stay with me"

The unmistakable sound of the stairs creaking brought all their attention quickly back and they watched as the light of the upstairs landing started to flicker. The creaking sound of the stair boards under weight continued to slowly ascend the staircase. In the flashes of the flickering light, Danny could see small puddles of water forming, starting at the bottom stair; a new little puddle appearing after each board creaked. They all stared in horror, and the icy chill that was creeping around their legs started to rise and engulf them. Danny's voice shocked them out of their trance. "Daisy, Emily, get what you need, we are going to mine."

The footsteps on the stairs ceased at his bellowing and the flickering light came on solid.

"Come on," Danny said again with urgency, "quickly get some things, we can come back here tomorrow. He was putting on his boots, then grabbed his coat and keys.

"What?" Daisy asked, terrified and half awake.

"What happened?" Emily asked grabbing her own and Daisy's coats.

"Quickly Daisy get your shoes on I will grab us clothes for the morning"

Once in the van Emily pushed Dan to explain.

"What happened in there Danny?"

"You guys can stay with me," Danny said, his voice rife with panic.

"Can you just tell us what's going on?" Daisy asked.

"There's something in that house," Danny spat out.

"I told you," Daisy boomed.

"What happened?" Emily demanded.

"Something knocked on the door," Danny started, "and I got up to go and see what was going on. I stood at the top of the stairs and someone or something pushed me down them."

"Pushed you? How?" Emily asked,

"I mean, I was standing at the top of the stairs, after I heard something knocking on the front door, and I felt something ice cold take a firm hold on my shoulder. I turned to see if it was you when the next thing I know, I was pushed hard, so hard my feet left the ground, and I was falling down the stairs. And then the water started to appear on the steps." Danny said, shaking his head.

"It's the man" Daisy said, "he's evil".

"It sounded like something was walking up the bloody steps, and every footstep, a little puddle of water would just form on the stair."

"Oh Danny, are you ok? Are you hurt? I've seen the water before too." Emily admitted.

"Mum, are you serious? You never mentioned that."

"I didn't want to scare you anymore than you already were," Emily replied.

"Something is definitely wrong in that place," Danny continued to shake his head, "I'm sorry I didn't really believe you."

"It's alright," Emily insisted, placing her hand on Danny's arm.

"When is the place getting cleansed or whatever," Danny asked.

"Two days," Daisy answered.

"My place is small," Danny stated, "but you guys are more than welcome to stay as long as you like. I'll even pay for a room if you want, but you can't stay there. I'll take you back in the morning to get some things."

"Thank you" both women replied in unison.

Danny's house was homely, warm and cozy. After hot cups of tea and some arranging of bedding on sofas and in a spare room, they all slept well. In the morning, they made a return trip, Emily gathering a few necessities, and Daisy quickly and nervously repacking all her belongings, with no intention of staying another night in the cottage. Her flight back to London had been booked for the day after the clearing. Two days went by quickly, and when they did return to the cottage again, it was to meet with Ruth and Debbie.

Danny waited in the van while Emily and Daisy walked Ruth and Debbie through the cottage.

"Oh my," Debbie uttered immediately upon

entering the little cottage, "do you feel the energy?" She asked Ruth.

"There's definitely some unsettled spirits here," Ruth confirmed, talking to Emily and Daisy.

"Are they good or bad?" Daisy quickly asked.

"Honestly, dear, a bit of both," Debbie answered.

"Who are they?" Daisy fired off.

"You'll have to give us a little while," Ruth answered kindly, "these things take time, even for the most practiced medium. Why don't you and your mum wait here," she motioned for them to sit on the couch in the small family room, "we'll let you know when we know what's going on."

Emily and Daisy nodded, taking their places on the small sofa as the two women moved about the house. They waited anxiously, listening to the women move out of one room and into another, and then back into the first room. They strained their ears, trying to make out what the women were saying to each other, but they spoke in soft, inaudible mumbles, sometimes to each other, and other times seemingly to themselves. The minutes felt like hours as the two mediums performed their work until, after nearly half an hour, Debbie and Ruth returned to the family room.

"Well," Debbie started, "I'm getting a very

strong reading with a man named Jack. Now, with all the research that you and Shelly did, we had found out that Jack had fallen from the light tower."

"Yes," Daisy added, "I have an article about it in the kitchen."

"What I'm getting from Jack," Debbie added, "is that he was pushed, murdered."

"Just like your dream," Daisy exclaimed looking at her Mum.

"You've dreamt this?" Ruth inquired.

"Yes," Emily answered, blushing, "I've had nightmares where I see this man, falling from the top of the lighthouse. In these nightmares, I always feel like he's pushed. Actually, it feels like I'm the one who's pushing him. I only recently realised that the man who fell in my nightmares was Jack, when Daisy brought that paper home with his picture."

"Interesting," Debbie added, "that makes sense."

"How?" Emily inquired.

"Often, in these situations, lingering spirits can try and show us truths in our dreams. It also makes sense that, if Jack was murdered, and it was believed to be an accident, his energy might get trapped here, in the physical world. Often, when these spirits become trapped, it can be attributed to unfinished business, of sorts."

"Poor man," Daisy chimed in.

"What's interesting," Ruth continued, "is that Jack's spirit isn't the only one here. We're both picking up on an older man, but he refuses to come out of the shadows. It's as if he's afraid of something."

"I have a pendulum with me," Debbie interrupted, "we're going to try and see if we can communicate better with that."

"How does that work?" Emily inquired.

"Well," Ruth answered, "we'll set up a place here in the cottage, somewhere quiet. We can use the pendulum to ask questions. Sometimes spirits are more open to communication through this method. Is there a certain place in the cottage where the activity has been especially heightened?"

"Bloody hell," Daisy blurted out, "I saw an old man in my room, when I first got here. Remember mum?"

"Of course," Emily nodded.

"Which room is that?" Debbie asked.

"At the top of the stairs," Emily stated, "the room on the left."

"Thank you," Ruth smiled, "being in close vicinity to where the spirit might reside can help us communicate better. We'll set up some things to help raise our spiritual awareness, candles and things like that. However, we will need complete quiet."

"We can wait outside," Emily stated.

"That would be lovely," Ruth replied, "thank you. We'll fetch you when we're done."

Emily and Daisy returned to the van, explaining what the women had told them about Jack, and how they had planned to try and communicate with the other spirit. The sun had set, and the three of them sat nervously outside, eyes glued to the little window in the room in which Daisy had stayed, watching the candlelight dance against the darkness. For thirty minutes they watched impatiently, and when the candlelight suddenly went out, and the window went dark, they figured that Ruth and Debbie must have finished their ceremony. In the matter of a few minutes, Ruth appeared at the front door, waving them back inside.

"How'd it go?" Daisy asked.

"It went well," Debbie answered, "the other spirit is that of a man named Blake."

"You and Shelly found some information on him as well, if I'm not mistaken," Ruth spoke to Daisy.

"We did," Daisy responded, "they thought that

he killed himself, after his wife disappeared and his really good friend Jack died."

"Right, right," Ruth nodded her head, "but we're getting a very different feeling from this spirit."

"Like Jack," Debbie added, "I'm getting very strong feelings that Blake was murdered as well. It does seem, though, that his spirit is much more spiteful and malevolent than that of Jacks."

"I don't think he was a great person in life," Daisy added.

"I think you're right," Ruth smiled.

"So, what do we do?" Emily asked.

Debbie cleared her throat, "I think that what we should do now, is perform a clearing. We'll treat the house with some white sage and try and speak with both spirits to convince them that they have no business here in the physical world."

"Will it work?" Emily asked, her voice hopeful.

Ruth placed her hand on Emily's shoulder, "all we can do is try."

"You have a train tomorrow, right?" Debbie asked Daisy, who nodded her head.

"Why don't you guys go get some rest," Debbie continued, "it might take several hours, there's no sense in you exhausting yourself here."

"Are you sure," Emily asked, "is there anything we can do to help?"

"Nothing at all dear," Ruth insisted, "Daisy, it was lovely meeting you, please don't be a stranger."

"I won't," Daisy answered, extending her arms to embrace Ruth. While the two hugged, Daisy whispered in Ruth's ear, "please don't let my mum come back here if this doesn't work."

Daisy felt the nodding motion of Ruth's head, and released her embrace, hugging Debbie with the same enthusiasm.

"Now you," Ruth looked at Emily, "get some rest, enjoy the little time you have left with your beautiful daughter. We'll call you tomorrow, ok?"

"Ok," Emily nodded, "but please, if you need anything, call me, ok?"

"Of course," Ruth assured.

Ruth and Debbie listened for the sound of Danny's large van pulling away before immediately setting to work with the ritual. The small cottage immediately filled with the strong smell of burnt sage, as the two moved throughout different parts of the cottage, each carrying a small, dried bundle, crackling as they slowly burned. The two women both repeated a variety of chants as they moved throughout the cottage, each saying things like: *It's time to leave this physical world that you are no longer bound to, and move into the light,* or, *you will never obtain the peace you seek here,* and, *a century has passed, there is no justice to be found now. The records will never be changed.* A litany of these phrases, and more like them, filled the cottage into the evening, accompanied by the lighting of more candles, and the continuous smoke from the sage, whirling its fragrance in smoky twists and turns. It was nearly two in the morning when the women finally snuffed out their sage bundles and left the cottage.

The next day, Emily and Danny took Daisy by the café, where they all had breakfast. Daisy said her goodbyes to Shelly, thanking her for her help, and insisting that they stay in touch. Daisy left for the station with her mum and Danny.

"Mum," Daisy said, her voice serious, "don't go back there unless they're certain everything is ok, please?"

"I won't," Emily laughed, "please call me as soon as you get to London, ok?"

"I will, mum."

"And don't worry about me, I'll be fine, I promise."

Daisy nodded and forced a smile, "let me know how it goes though, alright? I think the story from my break will top everyone's back at university!"

"I love you, mum," Daisy said, hugging her mum tightly, "and take care of her for me, won't you?", her eyes now directed at Danny

"Of course I will," Danny smiled "and it was great to have met you. I'll be looking forward to seeing you next time."

Daisy nodded, and headed for her platform, calling back one last time to her mum with a wave, "I love you."

CHAPTER
NINE

Jack spent the next few days reading and rereading the letter that Agnes had written to him, obsessing over things he could have done differently. If they had only moved a little bit quicker, they could have gotten her away; they were so close. He agonised over what might have become of her. As badly as he wanted to believe that she had somehow gotten herself away from this godforsaken lighthouse, and started a life somewhere new, he couldn't force himself to accept any scenario in which she wasn't dead, and he was certain it was at the hands of Blake. The question that scratched away at Jack's mind, even more it seemed, was the empty envelop Ben had received. Ben and Jack spent hours theorising over this, just as they did in the late hours of the evening, after Ben had finished his shift and was relieved by Blake, in Jack's cottage, sharing a bottle of whiskey.

"Maybe she just forgot to put the letter in the envelope," Ben said.

"She was smart," Jack would argue, "she wouldn't have just forgotten. Maybe Blake found them, and maybe there was just a little too much information. He could have removed it before she dropped them in the mail."

"Maybe," Ben would admit, "what did the inspector say about it?"

"The inspector considers it proof that she must have just run away," Jack said, dropping his head, "he says it's clearly a farewell address."

"Who knows," Ben replied, placing a hand on Jack's shoulder, "maybe that's exactly what it is."

"I don't think so, but I guess we'll never really know," Jack replied, defeated.

"I suppose not."

"What I do know," Jack said sternly, raising his head, "is that we need to get out of here. Blake is more unhinged than ever."

"There are other lighthouses out there," he continued, "there's other work, too, you just have to look."

"Look, just sit it out for a bit longer, ok?" Ben insisted.

"Ben," Jack's voice became serious, "Sarah and I have talked. We're leaving."

"When," Ben interrupted, surprised.

"In the next three days," Jack replied, "as soon as I collect my next wages."

"Where are you going?"

"We're leaving the island," Jack admitted, "I want you to come with us."

"You and Sarah love it here!"

"Not enough to continue in the employ of that lunatic," Jack snapped, "come with us. You know as well as I do that, he killed Agnes. God knows one of us might be next."

"We don't know that" Ben replied.

"Don't be a bloody fool," Jack raised his voice.

"I'm not leaving," Ben argued, "and you shouldn't either."

Just as Jack was about to launch his response, which had a litany of reasons why Ben should be leaving Anglesey with him and Sarah, he was stopped short by a sudden crack of thunder. The wind picked up with a force that made the little cottage creak and moan under the stress. Ben and Jack exchanged glances; between the booming claps of thunder, the faint sound of a voice yelling could be heard. Jack opened the door to his cottage; heavy rain drops whipping in and listened intently. He could hear his name being bellowed. Shielding his face the best he could, he walked into the storm, looking up at the light tower, immediately noticing the absence of the familiar rotating beacon of light. In the flashes of the blinding, purple lightening, he could make out the shape of Blake standing on the balcony, hands cupped round his mouth, screaming against the storm.

"Jack," he screamed again, "I need oil up here, now!"

"Alright," Jack called back, and hurried back to his cottage, knowing the importance of keeping the lighthouse beacon burning, especially in such a heavy storm.

Dripping wet, he entered the cottage breathless, Ben still sitting on his couch.

"Everything alright?" Ben asked.

"No," Jack managed between breaths, "you must have forgot to fill the lamp oil today. It's out."

"I didn't forget" Ben responded, "Blake told me he was doing it"

"Bloody idiot he is," Jack snapped back, "the light is out!"

"I'll take him some oil up then," Ben said apologetically.

"Don't worry about it," Jack said, pulling his heaviest wool coat on, "I'm already soaked anyway."

Before Ben could contest, Jack pulled the hood of his coat around his head tightly and disappeared into the storm, slamming the door behind him. Jack sprinted to the last cottage in the row of four, where they kept the supplies, and heaved a five-gallon metal bucket from a haphazardly stacked row. Jack quickly lugged the bucket towards the lighthouse, and up the stairs.

"Here," Jack exhaled, trying to catch his breath.

"Bloody took long enough," Blake snapped at him, muttering under his breath as he took up the weight of the bucket, "Ben, that bloody fool."

"What is that?" Jack exclaimed, pointing out at the ill-lit balcony.

"What the hell are you talking about?" Blake asked, squinting through the darkness.

A flash of lightening briefly illuminated the balcony, and both men saw, blowing in the wind of the storm, a white dress.

"It's Agnes," Blake yelled, as he began to move the oil bucket into an upright position, carefully as to not spill the highly flammable substance, "get out there!"

Jack quickly sprang into action, flinging the door open and stepping into the darkness of the balcony, barely able to keep solid footing on the slick metal grating. He reached the handrail, felt the roughness of the fabric in his hands as he held the empty dress, which appeared knotted tightly to the railing.

"What the hell?" He asked himself.

Just as Jack had turned around, his vision caught the shape of Blake's figure in the darkness, rushing towards him. He had barely got his arms raised up in an attempt to brace himself when Blake caught him. At full speed, and with all his weight, he shoved Jack over the railing. Jack grasped at the air, desperately attempting to grab something solid, flailing as he plummeted towards the ground. He wasn't even able to muster a scream before his body hit, with a loud, lifeless thud. Blake quickly untied the dress, and quickly hid it away, and sprinted down the long, spiralling staircase of the lighthouse.

Bursting from the door at the bottom of the lighthouse, he screamed in the most panic ridden voice he could muster, "Ben!"

Ben quickly threw the door of Jack's cottage

open, seeing Blake, with a terrified look on his face, "what is it?"

"It's Jack," Blake managed to spit out, "he's fallen."

Ben grabbed a small lantern and followed Blake into the storm, boots unlaced, sprinting around the base of the light tower. In the darkness, Ben stumbled, tripping on Jack's limp body.

"Jack! Jack!" He shouted repeatedly, shaking his body violently. He resorted to slapping Jack's face, pounding his chest, anything he could think of in his desperation. Despite all his efforts, Jack didn't respond. His body just lay, limp and heavy.

"He's dead," Blake said, placing his hand on Ben's shoulder.

"What happened?" Ben demanded.

"I don't know. He swore he saw some ropes or something loose in the wind. Said he had to tie them down. I couldn't see well, but he must have slipped."

Ben held the lantern up; Blake could see the doubtful look on Ben's face.

"You need to get up there," Blake said sternly, "and get that light burning again. Ships are going to need it in this bloody weather. I'll head to town and get the inspectors."

Ben held his scornful gaze, the rain hiding the

warm tears that ran down his cheeks. He thrust the lantern into Blake's hands, and silently made his way to the top of the tower. He distracted himself through the process of getting the massive lantern re-oiled and lit, the rotating beacon once again casting its light into the nothingness of the sea. He stayed in the tower, unable to bring himself back to the ground level, back to Jack. He walked the gallery and then the observation balcony, in search of whatever it might have been that led Jack to the railing. He found nothing. By the time Blake returned with the police and the coroner, the storm had subsided, and the sun was rising.

In the early morning light, from the top of the tower, Ben could see Jack's body, laying in a heap at the base of the tower, the grass surrounding his head, stained red from blood. When Ben reached the bottom of the lighthouse, Blake was talking to an inspector, who was jotting notes on a small pad; he remembered his face from when Agnes had gone missing.

"It was definitely the fall that killed him," the coroner said, rounding the base of the tower, and motioning for a few men that were with him to fetch the body.

"Like I was saying," Blake returned his attention

to the inspector, "he ran out onto that platform and must have slipped."

"Well," the inspector said, "certainly being drunk didn't help him."

"Right," Blake nodded.

"He wasn't bloody drunk," Ben interrupted.

"His breath reeked of whiskey," Blake challenged.

"I was with him all evening," Ben said intensely, "we had a few drinks, but he definitely wasn't drunk."

"How many drinks did you boys have?" The inspector asked arrogantly.

"A few," Ben answered solemnly.

"Right," the inspector responded, a smug look on his face, and jotted down more notes, "in any case, it seems pretty clear what happened here."

"I appreciate your work," Blake responded, a smile on his face, shaking the hand of the inspector before turning his attention to Ben, "you'll have to put in some extra hours until I can find a replacement up here, boy."

For the next two weeks, Blake and Ben worked back-to-back twelve-hour shifts, with Blake managing the tower during the day and Ben manning it by night. Blake drank more than he ever had, maintaining a perpetual state of inebriation. The two men hadn't spoken since the night of Jack's death. It was at the end of that second week when the picture became clear. Nearing the end of one of Ben's shifts, he removed the waste bag from the bin, intending to take it down the tower when he left. In doing so, he noticed some white fabric. Removing it from the bag, he realised it was a white dress. One that belonged to Agnes. It was still slightly damp, the sleeve of which had a rusty stain on it as if it had been tied to the rusty railings outside. It didn't take Ben long to piece together what had happened. Blake arrived moments later to Ben holding the dress up.

"Blake," Ben growled, holding up the dress to Blake's face, "what the hell is this?"

Blake eyed the dress, lighting his pipe, "it looks like a dress, boy. Are you dim?"

"I mean," Ben challenged, "why was it in the bin up here?"

"How the hell would I know?"

"It's Agnes' dress, isn't it?"

"It's not like I keep a list of everything she owned," Blake replied dismissively.

"It is," Ben asserted, "which means that it came

from your cottage. Why would you bring this up here?"

"Keep it up, boy," Blake challenged, his voice becoming serious, "and see what happens."

"I know what you did," Ben whispered.

"You don't know anything," Blake whispered back, "now get out."

Ben gritted his teeth and left. He wanted nothing more than for Blake to not exist, to move on, to disappear completely. Blake showed no signs of going anywhere soon, not on his own accord, anyway and he became unbearable. But, a few days after their confrontation, things changed drastically at the lighthouse. On a stormy, late autumn morning, the cliffs were being whipped by the sea, Ben found himself on the radio, calling the local rescue boat to the cliffside that the lighthouse stood on.

"This is Benjamin Campbell calling from lighthouse number three eight five. A man has fallen from the western face of the cliffs.

The lifeboat made haste arriving at the cliffside, but the churning waters were treacherous and there were no signs of Blake. The search was called off within an hour as the storm got worse and the crew's life was becoming endangered. Ben called the local authorities. The familiar arrogant inspector appeared at the cottages within a few hours.

"What happened?"

"I think he jumped," Ben stuttered.

"What do you mean jumped?" the inspector asked, shooting an untrusting look at Ben.

"I mean," Ben sobbed, "I mean I think he's killed himself."

"Why would a man of sound mind like Blake kill himself?" The inspector challenged.

"Sound mind?" Ben asked sarcastically, "the man's been bloody drunk around the clock. His wife has been missing for weeks, and two weeks ago one of his workers, I should say close friend, dies? That's a lot for any man to handle, sound mind or otherwise."

"I suppose," the inspector responded, "there's been a lot of bad stuff happened up here in these last few weeks. You best be careful up here, boy. The lifeboat crew will be out when the storm calms. but it will be to recover his body, no one could survive in that sea."

Three days later, the inspector reappeared at Ben's door.

"We're calling the search off," the man said,

"we're going to call it suicide, based on your testimony."

"It's very sad inspector, but I saw his decline after losing the two most important people in his life" Ben replied confidently, "I appreciate you keeping me informed."

"Right," the inspector stated, before turning his back and leaving.

THE SEARCH WAS OFF, and that was the last time that Ben would see the inspector. In the following days, he would be interviewed by the handful of small local papers that dotted the island. The interviewers would barrage him with questions about the tragedies that seemed to constantly plague the lighthouse over the last few months. He would answer their questions vaguely; Agnes went missing, Jack slipped from the tower, and the weight of the trauma was too much for old Blake to handle, and he claimed his own life in a drunken stupor, and it was all as simple as that. He never so much as hinted at how treacherous Blake was, or how he had suspected that Jack was pushed. When asked about Agnes' disappearance, he would simply shrug and make comments about how he was still hopeful she would someday return.

Within the month, Ben had applied and got the job as the head keeper of the new lighthouse at the other side of the island. He was tasked with hiring a new crew, which he quickly accomplished. A new life, a new start. Ben was just coming off one of his last shifts when he noticed one of the men tasked with clearing out Jack and Blakes cottages. He smiled wearily at the man, bidding him a good morning. Before retiring to his own cottage, Ben gazed out to the cold churning sea and prayed that he would be seen in the eyes of God as a good person. He hung his hat on the hook near the door, replayed every event in his mind, analysing everything that he could have done differently as he packed his own belongings, preparing for the move to the new lighthouse The guilt of Jack's death, though not his fault, plagued him more than the guilt of Blake's death ever could.

Ben would take the truth of what happened at the lighthouse to his grave, only three people knew the truth and perhaps Jacks ghost.

CHAPTER
TEN

"I wish we could have told him," Ben spoke aloud. "I know, I know," a voice called back, sympathetic and comforting, "it's not your fault. There's nothing you could have done."

"I don't know if I'll ever believe that" Ben called back, walking into the new cottage's kitchen.

"We should name him Jack," Agnes replied with a smile, rubbing her very swollen stomach.

BEN AND AGNES made the move to the new lighthouse quietly. While her sudden reappearance would have been easy enough to explain, neither had the desire to deal with the amount of attention this would give them. They didn't want to arouse the suspicion of the local authorities either. Keeping quiet was a skill that both had mastered in the year since they had fallen in love with one another; so quiet that the only suspicion Blake had of Agnes having an affair was with her close friend, Jack. Ben and Agnes settled in well to their new cottage, which was perched at the bottom of the new, state-of-the-art lighthouse, equipped with an electric light. The new cottage was larger, and, as stand-alone structures, they brought much welcomed privacy. Their lives were now like the fresh white paint that coloured the walls; pure and new, tarnished only by the regret of not acting quickly enough to save Jack's life.

"We should have told him," Ben could not let it go.

"You know we couldn't have risked that; the less Jack knew the safer he was," Agnes realised that was a stupid thing to say in hindsight. "Blake was unpredictable, you know that."

"Jack wouldn't have ever told him anything"

. . .

"But what if he did? Then all three of us would be dead," she paused, rubbing her stomach, "four of us."

"You know he was working on a plan to get you out of there," Ben said, dropping his head into his hands.

"I know, but it wasn't going to work, he would have been found out, we all would, and we all would have been killed. You did what you had to do Ben, for me and for your baby."

Agnes couldn't have said anything truer; Blake had killed Jack. While Jack was formulating a plan to get Agnes away, Ben had been working on his own plan. Ben had rented a small house on the very edge of the village, old and unassuming, at the end of a small street which had no reason for anyone to venture down. The night Agnes had gone missing, she had moved through the shadows of the night to this very house, where she could remain out of sight over the next few weeks. Ben's swearing that he had seen her on the cliff's edge was nothing more than redirection, a red herring. Ben knew that this would do a couple of things, the first being that it would create the idea that she likely had fallen from the cliff and was swallowed up by the ocean. The second being that, since he never stated actually seeing her fall from the cliff, it would be just as reasonable to assume she might have run away, which would resolve questions later when she suddenly reappeared. The plan had always been to smuggle Agnes away from the lighthouse, get rid of Blake, and for the two to live their years out together, with their soon-to-be-born child. Once Jack had decided to set things into motion to get Agnes away, they had resolved that Agnes would send a letter to Jack, and one to Ben, as a way of letting Jack know that she was still around. Of course, Jack took the letter to mean the opposite, and instead saw it as a sign that she knew she was going to be killed. Ben also didn't think of Jack being so insistent that he open his letter right then and there, thinking there would be no point in writing a letter, since Ben knew well where Agnes was, the empty envelope only further fueled Jack's paranoia, certain that Blake had somehow intercepted the letter, and discarded it.

IN THE MONTHS THAT FOLLOWED, Agnes maintained her low profile. Together, they had their first child, and named him Jack, in honor of their closest friend. When little Jack was 4 months old, and nearly a year had passed since all the chaos unfolded at the old lighthouse, Ben and Agnes arrived at the house of her parents.

"Agnes?" her father asked, dumbfounded by the sight of his daughter standing in his doorway.

"Yes, Father" she smiled, "it's me." She held up the baby, "and this is Jack."

"Mary!" John called, his eyes welling with tears of joy, "come quick!"

"What is it?" Mary called back grumpily but stopped dead in her tracks when she recognized her daughter's face, "my god, Agnes!"

"Mother," she smiled, "can we come in?"

"Of course, of course," her mother waved, "I knew you would come back"

"Jack, meet your grandparents"

"We have been waiting for your return ever since we got your letter," John managed to just get out the words before choking up."

Agnes explained to them how Ben had helped her runaway. She provided elaborate details on the beatings that she would take regularly at the hands of Blake, and how when he found out she was pregnant, he was decidedly certain of taking the baby's life or both together. She confessed about her affair with Ben, but only after divulging the details of Blake's drunkenness, womanising, and the abuse. She informed them that, had it not been for Blake's suicide, they likely would have never been able to return.

"I'm so sorry," John said, his eyes swollen from crying, "I should have never let you Marry that man."

"It's ok, dad," Agnes assured, "I don't blame you for anything. It kept you from losing everything. I would do it again."

"It's unforgivable," John moaned.

"Just be glad she's ok," Mary held John, "and Ben, I can't thank you enough for getting her out of there."

"If there's anything we can do," John added, "anything at all."

"Actually," Ben finally spoke, "there is."

"Anything," Mary said.

"I'm actually here to ask for your permission to Marry your daughter," Ben said joyfully, locking eyes with John.

"Ben," Agnes yelled with joy, "do you mean it?"

"There's nothing I could ever mean more," Ben replied with a smile.

"Do you love him?" John asked solemnly.

"More than anything," Agnes answered, hugging Ben tightly.

"Then of course you have my blessing."

The four of them exchanging hugs and handshakes. It wasn't long, and, despite the questions that they were all sure were going to come from the news of her return, they decided there would be a wedding. Agnes' mother was determined for it to be elegant this time, for it to be something magnificent, a way to try and give her what she was robbed of years ago. A union of love, not circumstance. The news of Agnes's return came, surprisingly, with very little excitement. Local authorities heard of the news quickly, and barraged both Agnes, and Ben, with the inevitable questions. She assured them that she had fled for the safety of her and her baby, and that Blake's suicide, tragic as it was, became the blessing that allowed her to stay where she loved, in Anglesey.

Beyond her parent's, and the interest of the police, there weren't many on the island who had a vested interest in her. The two of them lived out their years, Ben eventually moving past the guilt of

Jack's death, and Agnes bearing several more children, who would go on to have children of their own, one of whom became quite the well-known handyman in the small village that lay just a few miles from the old lighthouse.

CHAPTER
ELEVEN

After Emily had seen Daisy off at the station, she picked up Danny and they headed to Ruth's church, both equally anxious to find out if the Clearing was effective. Emily was exhausted and melancholy. Having mediums at her house, intended on Clearing its lingering spirits, and saying goodbye to her daughter, was nearly too much for her to bear in such a short span of time. More than anything, she hated that Daisy's visit had been riddled with so much stress. Danny pulled slowly down the gravel drive of the old brick building. When they were close enough that the church blocked out the sun, allowing their vision to be unhindered, they saw Ruth and Debbie standing outside, as if they knew they were coming.

"Hi," Emily called out, sounding as cheerful as she could as she exited the van.

"How did seeing off Daisy go?" Ruth asked sweetly.

"I don't think I'll ever get used to it," Emily admitted.

"Trust me," Ruth replied with a smile, "you never will."

"Well," Danny interrupted, "how did it go last night?"

"I think it went well," Debbie answered, "it seems the energy has quieted down."

"Thank you so much," Emily exclaimed excitedly, grabbing Debbie's hands in her own, "really, I can't thank you enough."

"We are glad to help," Debbie answered.

"So, she's ok to go back home?" Danny asked bluntly.

"I don't see why not," Ruth answered with a smile.

"Come by the cafe," Emily insisted, "please, anytime. Everything is on the house."

"Be careful," Ruth smiled, "we might just take you up on that."

"Please do," Emily beamed.

The four of them laughed together, and, after a

bit of small talk, went on their way. The sun was just setting over the bay when Danny and Emily arrived back at the lighthouse.

"Home sweet home," Danny laughed as he opened the door for Emily.

"Will you stay with me?" Emily asked, "I know they just did the Clearing, but I'd still feel a lot better if you did."

"Say no more," Danny smiled, "I would love to stay."

"Thank you."

"Do I get to stay in your room again?" Danny, asking half-jokingly.

"Of course," Emily winked, "I wouldn't want it any other way."

The two enjoyed an uninterrupted evening of wine and conversation in the cottage, which still bore the strong smell of burnt sage. A smell that lingered in the cottage for several weeks to come, a smell that Emily breathed in deeply every time she walked into the cottage, and exhaled slowly, with a smile of relief. Even with the new calmness that had fallen over the cottage, Emily never could feel comfortable staying alone. As the weeks became months, she found herself staying with Danny more and more frequently. On a night when a heavy winter snow was falling, and the two lay on the floor, the light from a small fire dancing over their still naked bodies, Danny posited a question.

"Emily," he asked seriously, "would you ever consider selling this cottage, and moving in with me?"

The room fell silent, the tension heavy in the air. Emily could feel Danny's body against hers, trembling with anticipation.

"I would love that," she finally whispered.

"We'd have to fix the place up a bit," Danny laughed,

"We'll start tomorrow," she smiled,

"Promise?" he whispered.

"Promise."

The next morning, Danny woke to the strong smell of brewing coffee, and the sight of Emily's face illuminated by the backlight from her laptop, her eyes glued to the screen.

"What are you looking at?" He asked, the coffee steaming from his mug as he poured it.

"I'm looking on Zoopla," she said, slightly puzzled, "you know this place has sold nine times in the last twelve years?"

"Wow," Danny said, equally puzzled.

"The last couple rented out the cottage too, as a Holiday let."

"Look it up," Danny said, "I bet you can still find the listing on some of those websites."

Emily found it, just as Danny thought, and she came across the address listed on a holiday rental website, with pictures of the antiquated cottages and towering lighthouse. She opened one of the pages, and scrolled to the reviews section, awe stricken by some of the comments that were left, she read aloud as she scrolled, "Coldest place I've ever stayed! We had to run the heating in the middle of the summer."

"Really noisy, there must be some type of animal living in the attic."

"Interesting cottage, historic place to stay, but definitely an eerie feeling, we were too uncomfortable to stay for the full week, strange water leaks everywhere, terribly unsafe."

"They just go on like this, Danny."

"You should have done your research before you bought the place," he laughed.

"Whatever," Emily replied with a playful hit on Danny's arm, "so where do we start, Mr. Handyman?"

"If it were me," Danny said, "the first thing I'd do

is a put an en-suite bathroom in the main bedroom, that's a huge selling point."

"How tough would that be?"

"It wouldn't be terrible," Danny assured, "it's doable, and probably the only real major overhaul the place would need. Other than that, a little sprucing up and I think you'd be in business."

"Alright," Emily smiled, "get to work then."

The first thing Danny had to do for the remodel is pull up a few of the floorboards in the main bedroom for the plumbing. The boards came up quickly and easily, but what Danny found underneath them was truly astonishing. There was a small book, some sort of diary and several envelopes, some with the name Agnes written on them, and others with the name Ben written on them. Danny slid a neatly folded letter out of one, skimming the page, before calling for Emily.

"What is it," she asked, breathing heavily from sprinting up the stairs.

"Look at this," Danny motioned to the pile of papers.

"What is all this?" Emily asked, beginning to thumb through the envelopes only briefly before exclaiming, "Oh my god, these are letters between Agnes and Ben, and a little diary I think!"

"Remind me again who they are," Danny laughed.

"They used to live in these cottages," she said, "Agnes was married to Blake, the head keeper, and Ben was one of the men who worked here under him, back in the twenties."

"Here," Danny gathered up all the little book and envelopes into a neat stack, laughing, "happy reading."

Emily took all of them and emptied the letters one at a time, carefully organizing them in chronological order, based on the dates that were written on the tops. Most of them were from Ben, addressed to Agnes. Some were written by Agnes; those, Emily assumed, were ones that she never got to him; the only logical explanation as to why they would be in her old cottage, and not his. Once the letters were organized, she began to read through them, and everything became clear.

One of the oldest letters, one that never made it to Ben, detailed how Agnes felt about him. In her writing, she rambled on about how much she longed for him, and how she wanted nothing more than to escape Blake and disappear for eternity with him. Emily was moved by the sweetness of her words. The diary was full of tiny writing, difficult to read but the horror was easy to pick out. It detailed the great duress she was under, and the physical and psychological abuse that she had been undergoing since nearly the onset of her marriage to Blake. Emily quickly put the pieces together, realizing that, in the nightmares, the ones where she saw Agnes terrified, it was of Blake. As Emily read on, she learned of the pregnancy, and of the fear of Blake claiming the life of her baby, of Ben's baby. She felt nauseous with that truth. When she came to the last of the letters Ben had written, she became deadly still, reading the letter out loud in a quiet whisper.

She called Danny to the kitchen, "Listen to this"

"*Agnes,*

You need to go now, you know where. Leave the pills under the stone, I'll get them after my shift. I'll come to you soon my love, just as soon as it's done. Move quickly and be sure no one sees you. They need to believe that you've disappeared or died. In a few weeks, he'll be dead, I will wait for the next storm which won't be too long I promise. It will all be worth it when you and our little one are safe. I swear that.

All my love,
Ben."

Just as Emily finished the letter, the dishes in the cabinet began to rattle violently.

"Danny," she screamed.

"What the hell?" he called out.

The cabinet doors slowly opened, and the dishes, one at a time, began falling, shattering on the floor. They both tried to catch the falling pates and slam the doors shut.

Suddenly everything stopped, they stood there in silence. Danny started to clear the shattered pottery.

"Go and pack Emily" he said.

Danny turned the ignition of his van. Emily sat quietly in the passenger seat. He took her hand in his, squeezing it tightly, "you'll never stay in there again. I promise."

He drove them to Emily's café, where Shelly poured them hot coffee and called her mum. Ruth arrived at the café within an hour, Debbie close at her heels.

"What happened dear," Debbie asked.

"We found these letters and a diary," Danny started, "under the floorboards in the master bedroom. Agnes must have slipped them between the cracks in the planks."

"Have you read them?" Ruth asked curiously.

"Some of the letters yes," Emily managed, "they were between her and Ben. They talked about their affair, how Ben planned to kill Blake, how the baby was his, how Agnes hid, letting everyone think she had died or ran away."

"Ok dear," Debbie interrupted Emily's rambling, patting her shoulder.

"Then the bloody dishes started breaking against the floor," Danny stated,

"When did that start?" Debbie asked.

"The second I finished reading the last letter to Agnes."

"Oh my," Ruth stated vaguely.

"What is it?" Emily begged.

"Well," Ruth started, "I supposed Blake wouldn't have known about the affair until you read the letter out to Danny"

"So what?" Danny asked.

"Well," Debbie interjected, "Emily reading those letters, Blake would have learned all of that for the first time. Wouldn't you be a tad upset, knowing that truth, especially after being trapped in the veil for so, so long?"

"What do we do now?" Danny asked.

"We'll try a stronger Clearing," Debbie chimed in.

"Fine," Emily stated, "that's fine. Do the strongest Clearing you can. I'm selling the place. That is, I'm done."

THE TWO WOMEN returned to the cottage and set to work immediately. They burned sage bundles, just as they had done before, and performed rituals using crystals and salt to purify the energy of the house. In similar fashion, they urged, and even demanded, that Blake let go of the physical world, abandon his anger, and leave in peace. The women heard heavy footsteps pacing the stairs, lights flickering throughout the cottage. In the guest room, where the women felt the energy was most focused, the strong smell of pipe tobacco overtook the scent of burning sage, and a large puddle of water forming at the foot of the bed. Then suddenly everything was peaceful and calm. The heavy atmosphere lifted, and the cottage felt at peace.

"It's done," Debbie exhaled.

In the morning, Ruth dialled Emily's number and informed her of everything they had done. When Emily and Danny arrived back at the cottage, if had a feeling of lightness and peace that they had never quite felt there. Even then, the two were anxious as they set to work sweeping the broken glass, and re-packing the few things that Emily had managed to unpack in the months since she had first moved in. Emily phoned an agent to list the property. Emily moved in with Danny, and the two made plans to turn the sale of the cottages into the purchase of a larger home for them to share; one that was well researched and free of any tragic past. The cottage was listed for a few weeks when Emily received a call from the agent.

"Emily, I have good news. We have an offer on the property."

"Oh, great," Emily breathed a sigh of relief.

"The thing is," the agent started, before Emily could get another word in, "it's ten thousand less than your asking price."

"Absolutely not," Emily insisted, "that's too low."

"I'll let them know," the agent responded happily, "by the way, have you guys been inside of the property lately?"

"Not since we've listed it," Emily said, curiosity in her voice, "why do you ask?"

"There's some water spots on the stairs, and in the bedroom" the agent replied, "and the electrics may need looking at, I was there on my own waiting for the viewers last night and the light in the hall started flickering and went out, I thought it may be the bulb but when the viewers arrived luckily it came back on. Good timing ay" the estate agent laughed

Emily shuddered.

"Actually, take the offer."

EPILOGUE

Emily and Danny sold the cottage, using the funds they purchased a run-down house, which sat overlooking the sea, just on the outskirts of the village. Emily did her research, as she promised herself she would, ensuring that the house wasn't the site of any tragedies. Danny set to work immediately, and within a few short months, the house was even more beautiful than Emily could have ever imagined it.

Emily and Danny still visited Ruth's spiritualist church on occasion, Danny had become a lot more interested in the "spirit world, since his experience. They inquired about how Shelly was doing. Shelly worked a few more months in the little café, but was never more excited than she was on the day that she left Anglesey, after she landed a job that would take her on extensive travels all over the world, including London on occasion, where she would always make sure to get together with Daisy and reminisce about the wild things that unfolded back at that little cottage.

Daisy continued with her studies, gradually working her way through a fine arts degree. In her visits with her mum, she had fallen completely in love with the island and was fully intent on opening her own gallery nearby her mum and Danny. Emily was counting the days.

Daisy was home for the summer holidays and visited her mum's coffee shop at the end of the day.

"Woah," Daisy exclaimed, as her mum came to sit with her.

"What is it?" Emily asked, startled.

"You'll never believe it," she insisted, sliding her phone across the table to her mum.

Emily studied the screen, awe washing over her face as she saw pictures of her old cottage on a holiday rental property website. "Wow, they have gutted the cottage! Taken out any character it had." The caption read: enjoy the beauty and privacy of this breathtaking cottage overlooking the Irish Sea. The cottage is the perfect getaway for a romantic trip. Located just outside of a lovely little village, full of interesting shops. Plan your Anglesey getaway today!

As she scrolled through the reviews, she shuddered at the comments, as recent as the weekend before, which detailed events that she was all too familiar with. She handed the phone back and shook her head, "the place just needs to be demolished." Her and Daisy shared a look.

"Well, at least it's not our problem anymore."

The End

Also by Charlotte Webb

The Haunting of Holly House

A Ghost Story

Meadowbank School for Girls is steeped in history, tradition, and whispers of a dark past.

As the Christmas term draws to a close, excitement buzzes through the boarding house—plays to write, parties to attend, and secrets lurking beneath the surface.

For Lizzy, Rosie, Emma and Dawn the task is simple: choose a prop, create a 20-minute play, and perform it before the school. But when they uncover a dusty Ouija board hidden beneath the stage, their innocent production turns into something far more sinister.

As they dabble with the supernatural, the line between make-believe and reality blurs.

Mysterious messages begin to emerge from the board, eerily connected to Holly House's dark past. Icy chills, unexplainable shadows, and terrifying encounters shake the girls' sense of safety. Strange occurrences aren't just coincidence—something malevolent has awakened.

Flashbacks to 1875 reveal a twisted love affair, a scorned housemistress, and a groundskeeper's dangerous obsession. And as Lizzy unravels the haunting story, she realises the ghost isn't a stranger at all—it's bound to her by secrets of the past.

In *"The Haunting Of Holly House"* secrets refuse to stay buried, and spirits won't rest until their story is told.

Gripping, atmospheric, and spine-chilling, this supernatural thriller will leave you questioning how far the past can reach into the present—and what happens when it refuses to let go.

Are you ready to discover who—or what—is pushing the glass?

Read Now - The Haunting of Holly House

About the Author

You are warmly invited to download Charlotte's first, free little book, and to connect with her on Facebook.

Here you can keep up to date with new releases and join in to chat about everything spooky and paranormal.

Ravencross Road (Download for free)

Facebook Page (Please like and follow)

Facebook Group - Charlotte's Haunted House

Charlotte Webb is a gifted author with a passion for all things paranormal. Her love for ghosts and the supernatural led her to run a business in the UK, taking curious thrill-seekers to haunted locations steeped in mystery. With firsthand experiences in some of the country's most eerie sites, Charlotte brings a vivid authenticity to her writing, drawing readers into chilling tales that feel all too real. Her books weave fact and fiction seamlessly, blending her encounters with an imagination that knows no bounds, offering readers a window into the worlds where shadows move, secrets linger, and the past never truly fades away.

Charlotte now resides in an old cottage in a small Northamptonshire village which is steeped in history and holds many ghost stories of its own. She shares her home with her husband, five rescue dogs, four parrots, and a lively flock of chickens and ducks. One of her books is set in this very home, and tells the story of a true ghostly character that has been seen many times in the countryside around her cottage.

Can you tell which is fact or fiction?

Printed in Great Britain
by Amazon